Error Analysis and Interlanguage

D1477743

Error Analysis and Interlanguage

S. P. Corder

Oxford University Press

Oxford University Press
Walton Street, Oxford OX2 6DP

London Glasgow New York Toronto
Delhi Bombay Calcutta Madras Karachi
Kuala Lumpur Singapore Hong Kong Tokyo
Nairobi Dar es Salaam Cape Town
Melbourne Auckland

and associates in
Beirut Berlin Ibadan Mexico City Nicosia

ISBN 0 19 437073 9

Set in Lasercomp Imprint by
Morrison & Gibb Ltd. Edinburgh

Printed in Great Britain at the
University Press, Oxford by
Eric Buckley, Printer to the University

Acknowledgements

Acknowledgements are made to the following publishers for permission to reproduce the papers in this collection:

Julius Groos Verlag, for 'The Significance of Learners' Errors', published in the *International Review of Applied Linguistics*, Volume V No. 4, 1967, for 'Idiosyncratic Dialects and Error Analysis', published in Svartvik, J. (ed.) (1973) *Errata: Papers in Error Analysis* and in the *International Review of Applied Linguistics*, Volume IX No. 2, 1971, and for 'The Elicitation of Interlanguage', published in a special issue of *IRAL* on the occasion of Bertol Malmberg's sixtieth birthday.

Centre for Information on Language Teaching and Research, for 'Describing the Language Learner's Language', published in *CILT Reports and Papers*, No. 6, 1971.

Cornelsen-Velhagen & Klasing & Co., for 'The Role of Interpretation in the Study of Learners' Errors', published in German as 'Die Rolle der Interpretation bei der Untersuchung von Schulfehlern' in *Fehlerkunde*, edited by G. Nickel, 1972.

HochschulVerlag (Germany), for 'The Study of Interlanguage', published in the *Proceedings of the Fourth International Congress of Applied Linguistics*, Volume 2, 1976.

Universität Bern and the Indiana University Linguistics Club, for '"Simple Codes" and the Source of the Second Language Learner's Initial Heuristic Hypothesis', published in *Studies in Second Language Acquisition*, Volume I No. 1, 1977, and for 'Language Distance and the Magnitude of the Language Learning Task', published in *Studies in Second Language Acquisition*, Volume II No. 1, 1978.

Université de Neuchâtel for 'Language Continua and the Interlanguage Hypothesis', published in the *Proceedings of the Fifth Neuchâtel Colloquium*, 1977.

The Association Finlandaise de Linguistique Appliquée, for 'Strategies of Communication', published in *AFinLA*, No. 23, 1978.

Newbury House Publishers Inc., for 'Formal Simplicity and Functional Simplification in Second Language Acquisition', published in *New Dimensions in Second Language Acquisition Research*, edited by Roger Anderson, 1980.

Contents

Introduction

There have always been two justifications proposed for the study of learners' errors: the pedagogical justification, namely that a good understanding of the nature of error is necessary before a systematic means of eradicating them could be found, and the theoretical justification, which claims that a study of learners' errors is part of the systematic study of the learners' language which is itself necessary to an understanding of the process of second language acquisition. We need to have such a knowledge if we are to make any well-founded proposals for the development and improvement of the materials and techniques of language teaching. These points are made in the first paper in this collection and developed in various ways in later papers. Roughly speaking one could say that the first half of the collection is concerned with the methodological problems of the study of errors and a consideration of the application of error analysis in second language teaching. The second group of papers on interlanguage is more concerned with theoretical problems, particularly those of second language acquisition and the nature of interlanguage, or the second language learner's language as a type of language and its relation to other language types. Thus the study of interlanguage has a purely theoretical value independent of its ultimate relevance to language teaching. It is part of the study of language or linguistics in its broader sense.

Until the late sixties when the first paper in this collection was written, the prevailing theory concerning the problem of second language learning was behaviouristic and held that the learning was largely a question of acquiring a set of new language habits. Errors were therefore predicted to be the result of the persistence of existing mother tongue habits in the new language. Most errors were ascribed to interference and consequently a major part of applied linguistic research was devoted to comparing the mother tongue and the target language in order to predict or explain the errors made by learners of any particular language background. What was overlooked or underestimated were the errors which could not be explained in this way. In any case, as far as teaching was concerned, all errors whatever their origin were dealt with by essentially the same technique of further drilling and exercise. The first paper in this collection dates to a time when this essentially behaviouristic account of second language learning was coming to be seriously questioned. This was the result of the interest which psycholinguists, influenced by Chomsky, were beginning to show in first language acquisition. It was natural that one should ask whether the cognitive processes which came into play in first language acquisition were the same as those used in second language learning, and indeed in the early seventies, which marked the beginning of serious empirical research into second language acquisition, this was the question which was uppermost in the minds of the researchers. With the general abandonment of the belief in a specific language acquisition device, this is no longer a question which actively engages the interest of investigators. At the same time the role of the first language in second language acquisition has become a more interesting question. The term *interlanguage* was coined by Selinker in the belief that the language learner's language was a sort of hybrid between his L_1 and the target language. The evidence for this was the large number of errors which could be ascribed to the process of transfer. But when second language acquisition researchers began to collect data from learners not receiving formal instruction, particularly children, the proportion of transfer errors was found generally to be quite small. Furthermore, these errors seemed to be found in most learners at the same stage of development and largely independent of the nature of their mother tongue. Clearly interlanguage was not a hybrid language and had a developmental history of its own. The speculation about a built-in syllabus for second language learning made in the first paper in this collection in 1967 seemed to be receiving empirical support. The notion of a 'natural sequence' for second language learning is now widely accepted with considerable support from experimental evidence. The relevance of these findings for language teachers is clear: that if we could establish the natural order in which a knowledge of the second language is gradually built up by the learner, then the materials, particularly the structural syllabus, could be graded upon a more solid basis than the current one, which is a mixture of some concept of usefulness and some idea of linguistic dependency, but certainly not on any psycholinguistic evidence of language learning.

While establishing the presence and nature of a 'natural sequence' of development may be the principal objective of second language acquisition research, the field has broadened out in its scope to include other topics. There has been in recent years a shift of emphasis in language teaching from a preoccupation with the learning of the language as a system towards the functional use of that system for communicative purposes. This has had its influence in second language acquisition research. There is now a greater awareness that under natural circumstances languages are acquired through the need and attempt to communicate, that is through conversation. But what is the nature of that conversation? Is it just like that between native speakers or does it have special characteristics? Native speakers of a language in fact adapt their use of language in a number of ways when interacting with learners and this is the data on which a learner works to create for himself his knowledge of the language system and its use in communication. But the learner is himself hampered in his attempt to use his interlanguage for communicative purposes by its relative simplicity and poverty. How does he overcome these disabilities? What strategies does he adopt to minimize the disabling effect of his ignorance? These too are topics dealt with in papers in this collection. An understanding of interlanguage is no longer narrowly bounded by a consideration of the structural properties; we also want to know the communicative circumstances under which it develops and how it is manipulated by its speakers in their attempts to communicate. We want to know these things because they too may be relevant to language teaching and learning.

1 The significance of learners' errors

When one studies the standard works on the teaching of modern languages it comes as a surprise to find how cursorily the authors deal with the question of learners' errors and their correction. It almost seems as if they are dismissed as a matter of no particular importance, as possibly annoying, distracting, but inevitable by-products of the process of learning a language about which the teacher should make as little fuss as possible. It is of course true that the application of linguistic and psychological theory to the study of language learning added a new dimension to the discussion of errors; people now believed they had a principled means for accounting for these errors, namely that they were the result of interference in the learning of a second language from the habits of the first language. The major contribution of the linguist to language teaching was seen as an intensive contrastive study of the systems of the second language and the mother tongue of the learner; out of this would come an inventory of the areas of difficulty which the learner would encounter and the value of this inventory would be to direct the teacher's attention to these areas so that he might devote special care and emphasis in his teaching to the overcoming, or even avoiding, of these predicted difficulties. Teachers have not always been very impressed by this contribution from the linguist for the reason that their practical experience has usually already shown them where these difficulties lie and they have not felt that the contribution of the linguist has provided them with any significantly new information. They noted for example that many of the errors with which they were familiar were not predicted by the linguist anyway. The teacher has been on the whole, therefore, more concerned with *how* to deal with these areas of difficulty than with the simple identification of them, and here has reasonably felt that the linguist has had little to say to him.

In the field of methodology there have been two schools of thought in respect of learners' errors. Firstly the school which maintains that if we were to achieve a perfect teaching method the errors would never be committed in the first place, and therefore the occurrence of errors is merely a sign of the present inadequacy of our teaching techniques. The philosophy of the second school is that we live in an imperfect world and consequently errors will always occur in spite of our best efforts. Our ingenuity should be concentrated on techniques for dealing with errors after they have occurred.

Both these points of view are compatible with the same theoretical standpoint about language and language learning, psychologically behaviourist and linguistically taxonomic. Their application to language teaching is known as the audiolingual or fundamental skills method.

Both linguistics and psychology are at the present time in a state of what Chomsky has called 'flux and agitation' (Chomsky 1966). What seemed to be well-established doctrine a few years ago is now the subject of extensive debate. The consequence of this for language teaching is likely to be far reaching and we are perhaps only now beginning to feel its effects. One effect has been perhaps to shift the emphasis away from a preoccupation with *teaching* towards a study of *learning*. In the first instance this has shown itself as a renewed attack upon the problem of acquisition of the mother tongue. This has inevitably led to a consideration of the question whether there are any parallels between the processes of acquiring the mother tongue and the learning of a second language. The usefulness of the distinction between acquisition and learning has been emphasized by Lambert (1966) and the possibility that the latter may benefit from a study of the former has been suggested by Carroll (1966).

The differences between the two are obvious but not for that reason easy to explain: that the learning of the mother tongue is inevitable, whereas, alas, we all know that there is no such inevitability about the learning of a second language; that the learning of the mother tongue is part of the whole maturational process of the child, while learning a second language normally begins only after the maturational process is largely complete; that the infant starts with no overt language behaviour, while in the case of the second language learner such behaviour, of course, exists; that the motivation (if we can properly use the term in the context) for learning a first language is quite different from that for learning a second language.

On examination it becomes clear that these obvious differences imply nothing about the *processes* that take place in the learning of the first and the second language. Indeed the most widespread hypothesis about how languages are learnt, which I have called behaviourist, is assumed to apply in both circumstances. These hypotheses are well enough known not to require detailing here, and so are the objections to them. If then these hypotheses about language learning are being questioned and new hypotheses being set up to account for the process of child language acquisition, it would seem reasonable to see how far they might also apply to the learning of a second language.

Within this new context the study of errors takes on a new importance and will I believe contribute to a verification or rejection of the new hypothesis.

This hypothesis states that a human infant is born with an innate predisposition to acquire language; that he must be exposed to language for the acquisition process to start; that he possesses an internal mechanism of unknown nature which enables him from the limited data available to him to construct a grammar of a particular language. How he does this is largely unknown and is the field of intensive study at the present time by linguists and psychologists. Miller (1964) has pointed out that if we wished to create an automaton to replicate a child's performance, the order in which it tested various aspects of the grammar could only be decided after careful analysis of the successive states of language acquisition by human children. The first steps therefore in such a study are seen to be a longitudinal description of a child's language throughout the course of its development. From such a description it is eventually hoped to develop a picture of the procedures adopted by the child to acquire language (McNeill 1966).

The application of this hypothesis to second language learning is not new and is essentially that proposed fifty years ago by H. E. Palmer (1917). Palmer maintained that we were all endowed by nature with the capacity for assimilating language and that this capacity remained available to us in a latent state after the acquisition of a primary language. The adult was seen to be as capable as the child of acquiring a foreign language. Recent work (Lenneberg 1967) suggests that the child who fails for any reason, i.e. deafness, to acquire a primary language before the age of 12, thereafter rapidly loses the capacity to acquire language behaviour at all. This finding does not of course carry with it the implication that the language learning capacity of those who have successfully learnt a primary language also atrophies in the same way. It still remains to be shown that the process of learning a second language is of a fundamentally different nature from the process of primary acquisition.

If we postulate the same mechanism, then we may also postulate that the procedures or strategies adopted by the learner of the second language are fundamentally the same. The principal feature that then differentiates the two operations is the presence or absence of motivation. If the acquisition of the first language is a fulfilment of the predisposition to develop language behaviour, then the learning of the second language involves the replacement of the predisposition of the infant by some other force. What this consists of is in the context of this chapter irrelevant.

Let us say therefore that, *given motivation*, it is inevitable that a human being will learn a second language if he is exposed to the language data. Study of language aptitude does in some measure support such a view since motivation and intelligence appear to be the two principal factors which correlate significantly with achievement in a second language.

I propose therefore as a working hypothesis that some at least of the *strategies* adopted by the learner of a second language are substantially the same as those by which a first language is acquired. Such a proposal does not imply that the course or *sequence* of learning is the same in both cases.

We can now return to the consideration of errors made by learners. When a two year old child produces an utterance such as 'This mummy chair' we do not normally call this deviant, ill-formed, faulty, incorrect, or whatever. We do not regard it as an error in any sense at all, but rather as a normal childlike communication which provides evidence of the state of his linguistic development at that moment. Our response to that behaviour has certain of the characteristics of what would be called 'correction' in a classroom situation. Adults have a very strong tendency to repeat and expand the child's utterance in an adult version; something like 'Yes, dear, that's Mummy's chair'.

No one expects a child learning his mother tongue to produce from the earliest stages only forms which in adult terms are correct or non-deviant. We interpret his 'incorrect' utterances as being evidence that he is in the process of acquiring language and indeed, for those who attempt to describe his knowledge of the language at any point in its development, it is the 'errors' which provide the important evidence. As Brown and Frazer (1964) point out the best evidence that a child possesses construction rules is the occurrence of systematic errors, since, when the child speaks correctly, it is quite possible that he is only repeating something that he has heard. Since we do not know what the total input has been we cannot rule out this possibility. It is by reducing the language to a simpler system than it is that the child reveals his tendency to induce rules.

In the case of the second language learner it might be supposed that we *do* have some knowledge of what the input has been, since this is largely within the control of the teacher. Nevertheless it would be wise to introduce a qualification here about the control of input (which is of course what we call the syllabus). The simple fact of presenting a certain linguistic form to a learner in the classroom does not necessarily qualify it for the status of input, for the reason that input is 'what goes in' not what is *available* for going in, and we may reasonably suppose that it is the learner who controls this input, or more properly his intake. This may well be determined by the characteristics of his language acquisition mechanism and not by those of the syllabus. After all, in the mother tongue learning situation the data available as input is relatively vast, but it is the child who selects what shall be the input.

Ferguson (1966) has recently made the point that our syllabuses have been based at best upon impressionistic judgements and vaguely conceived theoretical principles where they have had any considered foundations at all. The suggestion that we should take more account of the learner's needs in planning our syllabuses is not new, but has not apparently led to any investigations, perhaps because of the methodological difficulties of determining what the learner's needs might actually be. Carroll (1955) made such a proposal when he suggested it might be worth creating a problem-solving situation for the learner in which he must find, by enquiring either of the teacher or a dictionary, appropriate verbal responses for solving the problem. He pointed out that such a hypothesis contained certain features of what was believed to occur in the process of language acquisition by the child.

A similar proposal actually leading to an experiment was made by Mager but not in connection with language teaching (Mager 1961); it is nevertheless worth quoting his own words:

'Whatever sequencing criterion is used it is one which the user calls a "logical" sequence. But although there are several schemes by which sequencing can be accomplished and, although it is generally agreed that an effective sequence is one which is meaningful to the learner, the information sequence to be assimilated by the learner is traditionally dictated entirely by the instructor. We generally fail to consult the learner in the matter except to ask him to maximize the effectiveness of whatever sequence we have already decided upon.'

He points out as the conclusions he draws from his small scale experiment that the next step would be to determine whether the learner-generated sequence, or, as we might call it, his *built-in syllabus*, is in some way more efficient than the instructor-generated sequence. It seems entirely plausible that it would be so. The problem is to determine whether there exists such a built-in syllabus and to describe it. It is in such an investigation that the study of learners' errors would assume the role it already plays in the study of child language acquisition, since, as has been pointed out, the key concept in both cases is that the learner is using a definite system of language at every point in his development, although it is not the adult system in the one case, nor that of the second language in the other. The learner's errors are evidence of this system and are themselves systematic.

The use of the term systematic in this context implies, of course, that there may be errors which are random, or, more properly, the systematic nature of which cannot be readily discerned. The opposition between systematic and non-systematic errors is important. We are all aware that in normal adult speech in our native language we are continually committing errors of one sort or another. These, as we have been so often reminded recently, are due to memory lapses, physical states such as tiredness, and psychological conditions such as strong emotion. These are adventitious artefacts of linguistic performance and do not reflect a defect in our knowledge of our own language. We are normally immediately aware of them when they occur and can correct them with more or less complete assurance. It would be quite unreasonable to expect the learner of a second language not to exhibit such slips of the tongue (or pen), since he is subject to similar external and internal conditions when performing in his first or second language. We must therefore make a distinction between those errors which are the product of such chance circumstances and those which reveal his underlying knowledge of the language to date, or, as we may call it his *transitional competence*. The errors of performance will characteristically be unsystematic and the errors of competence, systematic. As Miller (1966) puts it, 'It would be meaningless to state rules for making mistakes'. It will be useful therefore hereafter to refer to errors of performance as *mistakes*, reserving the term *error* to refer to the systematic errors of the learner from which we are able to reconstruct his knowledge of the language to date, i.e. his *transitional competence*.

Mistakes are of no significance to the process of language learning. However, the problem of determining what is a learner's mistake and what a learner's error is one of some difficulty and involves a much more sophisticated study and analysis of errors than is usually accorded them.

A learner's errors, then, provide evidence of the system of the language that he is using (i.e. has learnt) at a particular point in the course (and it must be repeated that he is using some system, although it is not yet the right system). They are significant in three different ways. First to the teacher, in that they tell him, if he undertakes a systematic analysis, how far towards the goal the learner has progressed and, consequently, what remains for him to learn. Second, they provide to the researcher evidence of how language is learnt or acquired, what strategies or procedures the learner is employing in his discovery of the language. Thirdly (and in a sense this is their most important aspect) they are indispensable to the learner himself, because we can regard the making of errors as a device the learner uses in order to learn. It is a way the learner has of testing his hypotheses about the nature of the language he is learning. The making of errors then is a strategy employed both by children acquiring their mother tongue and by those learning a second language.

Although the following dialogue was recorded during the study of child language acquisition it bears unmistakable similarities to dialogues which are a daily experience in the second language teaching classroom:

Mother   Did Billy have his egg cut up for him at breakfast?
Child   Yes, I showeds him.
Mother   You what?
Child   I showed him.
Mother   You showed him?
Child   I seed him.
Mother   Ah, you saw him.
Child   Yes, I saw him.

Here the child within a short exchange appears to have tested three hypotheses: one relating to the concord of subject and verb in a past tense, another about the meaning of *show* and *see* and a third about the form of the irregular past tense of *see*. It only remains to be pointed out that if the child had answered *I saw him* immediately, we would have no means of knowing whether he had merely repeated a model sentence or had already learnt the three rules just mentioned. Only a longitudinal study of the child's development could answer such a question. It is also interesting to observe the techniques used by the mother to 'correct' the child. Only in the case of one error did she provide the correct form herself: *You saw him*. In both other cases, it was sufficient for her to query the child's utterance in such a form as: *You what?* or *You showed him?* Simple provision of the correct form may not always be the only, or indeed the most effective, form of correction since it bars the way to the learner testing alternative hypotheses. Making a learner try to discover the right form could often be more instructive to both learner and teacher. This is the import of Carroll's proposal already referred to.

We may note here that the utterance of a correct form cannot be taken as proof that the learner has learnt the systems which would generate that form in a native speaker, since he may be merely repeating a heard utterance, in which case we should class such behaviour, not as language, but in Spolsky's term (Spolsky 1966) 'language like behaviour'. Nor must we overlook the fact that an utterance which is superficially non-deviant is not evidence of a mastery of the language systems which would generate it in a native speaker since such an utterance must be semantically related to the situational context. The learner who produced 'I want to know the English' might have been uttering an unexceptionable sentiment, but it is more likely that he was expressing the wish to know the English language. Only the situational context could show whether his utterance was an error or not.

Although it has been suggested that the strategies of learning a first and second language may be the same, it is nevertheless necessary at this point to posit a distinction between the two. While one may suppose that the first language learner has an unlimited number of hypotheses about the nature of the language he is learning which must be tested (although strong reasons have been put forward for doubting this) we may certainly take it that the task of the second language learner is a simpler one: that the only hypotheses he needs to test are: 'Are the systems of the new language the same or different from those of the language I know? And if different, what is their nature?' Evidence for this is that a large number, but by no means all, of his errors, are related to the systems of his mother tongue. These are ascribed to interference from the habits of the mother tongue, as it is sometimes expressed. In the light of the new hypotheses they are best not regarded as the persistence of old habits, but rather as signs that the learner is investigating the systems of the new language. Saporta (1966) makes this point clear, 'The internal structure of the (language acquisition) device, i.e., the learner, has gone relatively unexplored except to point out that one of its components is the grammar of the learner's native language. It has generally been assumed that the effect of this component has been inhibitory rather than facilitative'. It will be evident that the position taken here is that the learner's possession of his native language is facilitative and that errors are not to be regarded as signs of inhibition, but simply as evidence of his strategies of learning.

We have been reminded recently of von Humboldt's statement that we cannot really teach language, we can only create conditions in which it will develop spontaneously in the mind in its own way. We shall never improve our ability to create such favourable conditions until we learn more about the way a learner learns and what his built-in syllabus is. When we do know this (and the learner's errors will, if systematically studied, tell us something about this) we may begin to be more critical of our cherished notions. We may be able to allow the learner's innate strategies to dictate our practice and determine our syllabus; we may learn to adapt ourselves to *his* needs rather than impose upon him *our* preconceptions of *how* he ought to learn, *what* he ought to learn and *when* he ought to learn it.

2 Idiosyncratic dialects and error analysis

What has come to be known as 'error analysis' has to do with the investigation of the language of second language learners. I shall be taking the point of view in this chapter that the language of such a learner, or perhaps certain groupings of learners, is a special sort of dialect. This is based on two considerations: firstly, any spontaneous speech intended by the speaker to communicate is meaningful, in the sense that it is systematic, regular, and consequently is, in principle, describable in terms of a set of rules, i.e., it has a grammar. The spontaneous speech of the second language learner is language and has a grammar. Secondly, since a number of sentences of that language are isomorphous with some of the sentences of his target language and have the same interpretation, then some, at least, of the rules needed to account for the learner's language will be the same as those required to account for the target language. Therefore the learner's language is a dialect in the linguistic sense: two languages which share some rules of grammar are dialects.

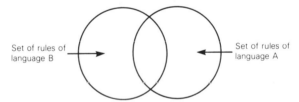

Set of rules of language B

Set of rules of language A

Language A and B are in a dialect relation. (I am not here concerned whether or not all languages can be regarded as being in this relation.)

It is, of course, usual to apply a further non-linguistic criterion to a language in order to establish its dialect status, namely that it should be the shared behaviour of a social group, i.e., that it should constitute a 'langue' in the de Saussurean sense. In this sense the language of a learner may or may not be a dialect. I shall return to this point later. For the time being, however, I shall make a distinction between the dialects which are the languages of a social group (I shall call these social dialects) and the dialects which are not the languages of social groups (I shall call these idiosyncratic dialects). The justification for calling the latter dialects is therefore a linguistic one and not a social one. You may say that the dialects I am talking about are already adequately identified under the name *idiolects*. I would maintain that this is not the case. An idiolect is a personal dialect but one which linguistically has the characteristic that all the rules required to account for it are found somewhere in the set of rules of one or another *social* dialect. An *idiolect* can be said to be some sort of a mixture of dialects.

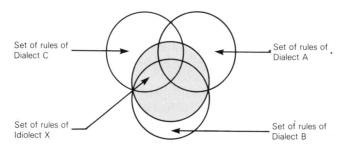

From the diagram we can see that Idiolect X possesses rules drawn from three overlapping social dialects but does not possess any rules which are not rules of any one of these dialects. If all these social dialects are 'included' in a language D then Idiolect X is a dialect of language D in the conventional sense.

This state of affairs is different in the case of what I am calling idiosyncratic dialects. In these, some of the rules required to account for the dialect are not members of the set of rules of any social dialect; they are peculiar to the language of that speaker.

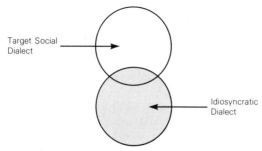

All *idiosyncratic dialects* have this characteristic in common that some of the rules required to account for them are particular to an individual. This has, of course, the result that some of their sentences are not readily interpretable, since the ability to interpret a sentence depends in part upon the knowledge of the conventions underlying that sentence. The sentences of an *idiolect* do not therefore present the same problems of interpretation since somewhere there is a member of that social group who shares the conventions with the speaker.

It is in the nature of idiosyncratic dialects that they are normally unstable. The reason for this is obvious. The object of speech is normally to communicate, i.e., to be understood. If understanding is only partial, then a speaker has a motive to bring his behaviour into line with conventions of some social group, if he is able. This instability accounts for part of the difficulty experienced by the linguist in describing idiosyncratic dialects. The data on which a description is made is fragmentary. This means that the usual verification procedures required in the construction of a projective grammar are not readily available.

The other difficulty the linguist experiences is that of placing an interpretation on some of the sentences of the dialect. Without interpretation, of course, analysis cannot begin.

The language of a second language learner is not the only type of idiosyncratic dialect. 'Error analysis' is not applicable only to the language of second language learners. One class of idiosyncratic dialects is the language of poems, where this cannot be accounted for wholly in the terms of the rules of some social dialect. As Thorne (1965) says: 'given a text like Cummings' poem "Anyone lived in a pretty how town" containing sequences which resist inclusion in the grammar of English, it might prove more illuminating to regard it as a sample of a different language, *or a different dialect*, from standard English' (my italics).

That the language of this poem is idiosyncratic is evident, if only because of the difficulty of interpretation. It is significant that Thorne's approach to the analysis of the language of the poem is essentially that of 'error analysis', a type of bilingual comparison. That is, he attempts to discover the rules which would account for the idiosyncratic sentences in terms of the same syntactic model he uses to account for the social dialect to which it most closely relates: in this case, standard English.

The idiosyncratic sentences of a poetic text can perhaps with justice be called *deliberately deviant*, since the author presumably knows the conventions of the standard dialect but chooses not to obey them (cf. Katz 1964). His deviances are motivated. This means that the ability to interpret the text is dependent upon the knowledge of the semantic structure of the related standard dialect. In this sense poetic dialects are 'parasitic' upon standard dialects.

Another idiosyncratic dialect one might consider is the speech of an aphasic. This, too, in the happiest circumstances, is an unstable dialect, but presents the same problem of interpretation to the linguist. Whether it would be just to call the idiosyncratic sentences of an aphasic deviant is, however, less certain. We must assume that he was, before his disease, a native speaker of some social dialect, but he cannot be said to be deviating deliberately, and it is difficult to know in what sense he can be said still to 'know the rules' of the dialect.

Perhaps we may provisionally characterize the idiosyncratic sentences of the aphasic as *pathologically deviant*.

The third class of idiosyncratic dialects is that of the infant learning his mother tongue. It too presents typical problems of interpretation, in an even more acute form perhaps than either of the other two classes. I am open to correction here, but I would guess that the single factor which makes the problem of describing child language so intractable is that of placing a plausible interpretation (let alone a correct interpretation) upon a child's utterances. This idiosyncratic dialect is also obviously unstable.

The fourth class of idiosyncratic dialects is that of the learners of a second language. Everything I have said about idiosyncratic dialects in general applies to his language. It is regular, systematic, meaningful, i.e., it has a grammar, and is, in principle, describable in terms of a set of rules, some sub-set of which is a sub-set of the rules of the target social dialect. His dialect is unstable (we hope) and is not, so far as we know, a 'langue' in that its conventions are not shared by a social group (I shall return to this point later), and lastly, many of its sentences present problems of interpretation to any native speaker of the target dialect. Selinker (1972) has proposed the name *interlanguage* for this class of idiosyncratic dialects, implying thereby that it is a dialect whose rules share characteristics of two social dialects of languages, whether these languages themselves share rules or not. This is an open question and has to do with the problem of language universals.

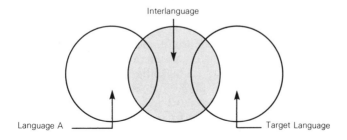

Interlanguage

Language A   Target Language

An alternative name might be *transitional dialect*, emphasizing the unstable nature of such dialects.

I have suggested that it would be reasonable to call the idio-syncratic sentences of a poet's dialect *deliberately deviant*, since the writer is assumed to know the conventions of a social dialect, and that he deliberately chooses not to follow them. Similarly I have suggested that the aphasic's idiosyncratic sentences might be called *pathologically deviant* since he too was presumably a speaker of some social dialect before his disease. We cannot, however, refer to the idiosyncratic sentences of a child as deviant, since he, of course, is not yet a speaker of a social dialect; and indeed it is not usual (until he goes to school) to call a child's sentences deviant, incorrect, or ungrammatical. For precisely the same reason I suggest it is misleading to refer to the idiosyncratic sentences of the second language learner as *deviant*. I also suggest that it is as undesirable to call them *erroneous* as it is to call the sentences of a child erroneous, because it implies wilful or inadvertent breach of rules which, in some sense, ought to be known. Whereas, of course, sentences are idiosyncratic precisely because the rules of the target dialect are not yet known.

The only sentences in anyone's speech which could, I suggest, with justice be called *erroneous* are those which are the result of some failure of performance. These may contain what are often called slips of the tongue, false starts, changes of mind, and so on. Hockett (1948) refers to these as 'lapses'. They may be the result of failures in memory. A typical example in English would be: 'That is the problem which I don't know how to solve it' (Reibel 1969). Interestingly such erroneous sentences do not normally present problems of interpretation. The reason that suggests itself for this is that there may be, in any social dialect, 'rules for making mistakes'. Here, clearly, is a field for investigation (Boomer and Laver 1968). But we are not yet in a position, I think, to set up a fifth class of idiosyncratic dialects to account for the regularities of erroneous sentences. The noticeable thing about *erroneous* sentences is that they are normally readily corrected or correctable by the speaker himself. This could be a defining criterion for erroneous sentences. It would, of course, be applicable to some sentences of the second language learner. Such sentences could be accounted for as being cases of *failure* (for whatever reason) to follow a *known* rule, in contradistinction to what I am calling idiosyncratic sentences, which involve no failure in performance and which cannot be corrected by the learner precisely because they follow the only rules known to him, those of his transitional dialect.

But so long as we do not make the mistake of assuming that the idiosyncratic sentences of a learner of a second language are simply the result of performance failure, that is, that he knows the rules of the target language but has, for some reason or other failed to, or chosen not to, apply them, then there is no harm in talking about *error* or *correction*.

My principal reason for objecting to the terms *error*, *deviant*, or *ill-formed* is that they all, to a greater or lesser degree, prejudge the explanation of the idiosyncrasy. Now, one of the principal reasons for studying the learner's language is precisely to discover why it is as it is, that is, to explain it and ultimately say something about the learning process. If, then, we call his sentences deviant or erroneous, we have implied an explanation before we have ever made a description.

There is an even more compelling reason for not calling the idiosyncratic sentences of a learner *ungrammatical*. While it is true that they cannot be accounted for by the rules of the target dialect, they are in fact *grammatical* in terms of the learner's language.

I have suggested that the idiosyncratic dialects I have identified differ from social dialects in that some of the rules needed to account for them are not members of the set of rules of any social dialect, that they are in fact idiosyncratic rules, not shared rules. It is, however, possible that while these dialects are not 'langues', in the sense that their conventions are not shared by any social group identifiable according to the criteria of the sociologist, nevertheless the idiosyncratic rules are not unique to an individual but shared by others having similar cultural background, aims or linguistic history. There is such a term as 'poetic language' or 'poetic dialect' to designate that dialect which possesses certain features found only in poetry. However, such a dialect is part of the 'langue' of the community whose poetry it is and presents no difficulties of interpretation. Such a sentence as: 'And hearkened as I whistled the trampling team beside' is perhaps unique to verse in modern English but can be accounted for by a convention accepted by all English speakers. This is not true, however, of 'Up so many bells . . .' of Cummings' poem. This is not part of the poetic dialect of English, is difficult of interpretation and I doubt whether the rules which accounted for it would account for any other poetic utterances by any other poet. It is fully idiosyncratic.

The situation is, I think, different in the case of the other three classes of idiosyncratic dialects. Aphasics do not form a social group in any sociological sense, and yet there is strong evidence to suggest that the idiosyncrasies of their speech may be classified along a number of dimensions (Jakobson 1956). No one would, of course, attempt to describe the speech of aphasics unless he believed that

some general statements of classification were possible. The object
of such investigations is to find what relations there are between the
medical signs, symptoms, history, and the set of rules needed to
account for the idiosyncratic aspects of the aphasic's speech.

Similarly, no one would undertake the study of child language
acquisition unless he had reason to believe that all children in a
certain dialect environment followed a course of development
which was more or less similar (Smith and Miller 1966). There
would be little point in describing the speech of *a* three-year-old
unless it was expected ultimately to throw light on the speech of *the*
three-year-old. Therefore, there is an underlying assumption that
the language of all three-year-olds in a certain language environment will have certain features in common.

May it be that the situation is similar in the case of the learner of a
second language? It is certainly the case that teachers work on the
assumption that a group of learners having the same mother tongue
and having had the same experience of learning the second language
speak more or less the same interlanguage at any point in their
learning career, and that what differences there are can be ascribed
to individual variation in intelligence, motivation, and perhaps
attitude. This belief is inherent in the notion of 'teaching a class' as
opposed to an 'individual', and indeed, it is difficult to see how one
could proceed otherwise.

Can we assume that such learners all follow a similar course of
development in acquiring a second language? We certainly do all we
can to see that they do. That is what a syllabus is for. It is a map of
the route the learners are to follow. But supposing it were possible
for the learner to select his own route, can we assume that he would
follow the route we have mapped out for him? We simply do not
know, since no one has ever tried to find out. We lack totally any
information about the development of individual learners of a
second language outside the classroom situation, and indeed it is
difficult to imagine how such a study could be made. But one thing is
clear: the longitudinal study of the language development of a
second language learner would rely heavily upon the techniques of
what we are calling 'error analysis' just as the longitudinal study of
the infant learning his mother tongue depends on the analysis of his
idiosyncratic sentences (Brown and Frazer 1964). Furthermore, I
believe that until we do attempt to undertake the longitudinal study
of the free-learning second language learners, we shall not make
much headway with finding out how people learn second languages.

I shall now turn to a general consideration of the methodology of
describing what I have called an idiosyncratic dialect, and which, in
part, is 'error analysis' as we are calling it. I have already suggested

that this methodology is not uniquely applicable to the dialects of second language learners but is valid for all idiosyncratic dialects.

The dialect is *une langue* in the de Saussurean sense. It is therefore a methodological mistake to concentrate only on those sentences which are overtly idiosyncratic. The superficially well-formed sentences in terms of one social dialect (the target dialect in the case of the learner) are just as important as those which are overtly idiosyncratic. They too tell us what he knows. Furthermore, as I have suggested above, the 'value' to be assigned to 'well-formed' forms is only discoverable in terms of the whole system of his dialect. Thus, for example, a well-formed 'plural' or an apparently 'proper' use of the definite article can only be understood in relation to his 'ill-formed' plurals or his use of other determiners.

This means that all the learner's sentences should in principle be analysed. This is all the more necessary since many of his apparently 'well-formed' sentences may have a derivation different from that assigned by the rules of the target dialect. Thus the sentence: 'After an hour it was stopped' was only recognized as idiosyncratic when the context showed that *it* referred to the *wind* and that therefore the target dialect interpretation was unlikely and in fact the translation into the target language was: 'After an hour it stopped'. A similar case in poetic dialect is: 'Anyone lived in a pretty how town' where the syntactic parallel is not with 'Someone lived in a pretty old town' but 'John lived in a pretty old town', i.e., *Anyone* is a proper name in that poetic dialect, and not an indefinite pronoun, and *how* is an adjective and not an interrogative adverb.

The first stage in 'error analysis' then is *recognition of idiosyncracy*. We can enunciate a general law. *Every sentence is to be regarded as idiosyncratic until shown to be otherwise.* As I have suggested, a learner's sentence may be superficially 'well-formed' and yet be idiosyncratic; these sentences I shall call *covertly idiosyncratic*. They may also, of course, be *overtly idiosyncratic*, in that they are superficially 'ill-formed' in terms of the rules of the target language, or they may, of course, be neither. If the 'normal' interpretation is acceptable in context, then that sentence is not for immediate purposes idiosyncratic. If, however, the sentence appears superficially well-formed in terms of the rules of the target language but nevertheless cannot be interpreted 'normally' in context, then that sentence is *covertly idiosyncratic* and a plausible interpretation must be placed upon it in the light of the context. We then have what I call a *reconstructed sentence* to compare with the original. A reconstructed sentence is, roughly speaking, what a native speaker of the target language would have said to express *that* meaning in *that* context, i.e., it is a translation equivalent.

Let us take another possibility: that the sentence is *overtly idiosyncratic*, that is, it is superficially 'ill-formed' according to the rules of the target language. We must then ask whether a plausible interpretation can be placed upon it in the context. If it can, well and good, and we can proceed to make a 'well-formed' reconstructed sentence to compare with the original. If we cannot readily make a plausible interpretation of the overtly idiosyncratic sentence then our problem is much greater. Somehow or other we must attempt to make a plausible interpretation. We can first see whether, by reference to the mother tongue of the learner, we can arrive at such an interpretation. If the mother tongue is not known then the analysis of that sentence may have to remain in abeyance until we have learnt more of the idiosyncratic dialect of the learner. If, however, the mother tongue is known, we may be able, by a process of literal translation, to arrive at a means of interpreting the sentence plausibly. If we can do that, then, by translating the mother tongue sentence back into a well-formed sentence of the target language, we have available a reconstructed sentence which once again we can compare with the original overtly idiosyncratic sentence of the learner.

The end point of the process of identifying idiosyncracy and the production of a reconstructed sentence is two sentences: the idiosyncratic sentence and a well-formed sentence, which *by definition* have the same meaning.

I need hardly say that the picture I have given is idealized. At every decision point in the algorithm it is unlikely that a categorical 'yes/no' answer can readily be made. The first decision as to the 'well-formedness' is in itself a problem in view of the indeterminacy of grammar (Lyons 1968). But more acute is the problem of interpretation. How can we be sure when interpretation is plausible? Frequently there may be two equally plausible interpretations. Take for example such an overtly idiosyncratic sentence as: *He didn't know the word so he asked a dictionary*. In the context the interpretation *He asked for a dictionary* is perhaps as likely as *He consulted a dictionary*. There is not always in the context any factor which will make one interpretation more plausible than another. Recourse can often be had to the mother tongue, if known. But I think it worth pointing out that the problem of interpretation looms larger outside the classroom than in. The teacher has almost certainly learnt the idiosyncratic dialect of his class and, of course, there is always the possibility of asking the learner in his mother tongue to provide an authoritative interpretation.

The recourse to the mother tongue of the learner (in his absence,

Algorithm for providing data for description of idiosyncratic dialects

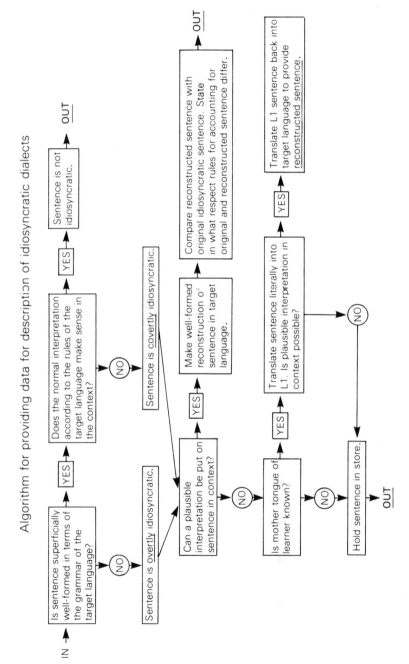

that is) is in fact also a highly intuitive process and, of course, depends on the degree of knowledge of that dialect possessed by the investigator. Furthermore, we cannot assume that the idiosyncratic nature of the learner's dialect is solely explicable in terms of his mother tongue; it may be related to how and what he has been taught. Here again the teacher is in a privileged position to interpret the idiosyncratic sentence, though teachers may be unwilling to admit that idiosyncracy can be accounted for by reference to what they have done or not done!

We have now arrived at the second stage: *accounting for a learner's idiosyncratic dialect.* The first stage, if successfully completed, provides us with the data of a set of pairs of sentences which by definition have the same meaning, or put another way, are translation equivalents of each other: one in the learner's dialect, the other in the target dialect. This is the data on which the *description* is based. The methodology of description is, needless to say, fundamentally that of a *bilingual comparison.* In this, two languages are described in terms of a common set of categories and relations, that is, in terms of the same formal model. The technical problems of this are well known and I do not wish, or need, to go into them here.

The third stage and ultimate object of error analysis is *explanation.* Whereas the two previous stages have been linguistic, the third stage is psycholinguistic, in as much as it attempts to account for how and why the learner's idiosyncratic dialect is of the nature it is. We must, I think, all agree that there could be no reason to engage in error analysis unless it served one or both of two objects. Firstly, to elucidate what and how a learner learns when he studies a second language. This is a theoretical object; secondly, the applied object of enabling the learner to learn more efficiently by exploiting our knowledge of his dialect for pedagogical purposes. The second objective is clearly dependent on the first. We cannot make any principled use of his idiosyncratic sentences to improve teaching unless we understand how and why they occur.

It is a generally agreed observation that many – but not necessarily all – the idiosyncratic sentences of a second language learner bear some sort of regular relation to the sentences of his mother tongue.

This is a phenomenon which no one would dispute. It is the explanation of this phenomenon which is open to discussion. One explanation is that the learner is carrying over the habits of the mother tongue into the second language. This is called *interference* and the implication of this term can only be that his mother tongue habits prevent him in some way from acquiring the habits of the second language. Clearly this explanation is related to a view of language as some sort of habit structure.

The other explanation is that language learning is some sort of data-processing and hypothesis-forming activity of a cognitive sort. According to this view his idiosyncratic sentences are signs of false hypotheses, which, when more data is available and processed, either by direct observation or by statements by the teacher, i.e., corrections and examples, enable the learner to reformulate a hypothesis more in accordance with the facts of the target language (Hockett 1948).

It is not surprising that people holding the habit-formation theory of learning, which has been the most prevalent theory over some decades now, showed no particular interest in the study of the learner's idiosyncratic sentences. They were evidence that the correct automatic habits of the target language had not yet been acquired. Their eradication was a matter of more intensive drilling in correct forms. What the nature of the error might be was a matter of secondary importance since it would throw no interesting light on the process of learning. Sufficient that they were there, indicating that the learning task was not yet complete. Theoretically, if the teaching process had been perfect, no errors would have occurred.

The alternative view would suggest that the making of errors is an inevitable and indeed necessary part of the learning process. The 'correction' of error provides precisely the sort of negative evidence which is necessary to discovery of the correct concept or rule. Consequently, a better description of idiosyncratic sentences contributes directly to an account of what the learner knows and does not know at that moment in his career, and should ultimately enable the teacher to supply him, not just with the information that his hypothesis is wrong, but also, importantly, with the right sort of information or data for him to form a more adequate concept of a rule in the target language.

It is not, I think, therefore, a pure coincidence that an increased interest in error analysis at the present time coincides with an increased interest in formulating some alternative hypothesis to the habit-formation theory of language learning.

3 Describing the language learner's language

Improvements in the methods and materials of second language teaching are likely to remain a matter of trial and error until we have a better understanding than we have at present of the processes of learning a second language. The amount of research in this field is small and the results disappointing. Too much has been piecemeal and too much operational and local in its validity. We need a more general and pure attack on the problem. The suggestion that has frequently been repeated, that language learning is some obscure and little understood process of data processing, is a potentially fruitful one likely to benefit from the now increasing amount of work done in the psychology of cognition. The analogy often proposed for language learning is couched in terms of computer terminology – data processing, input, output, operations, and so on. On this analogy the data of the target language to which the learner is exposed represents the input; the learning process, the data-processing operation, and the output a grammar of the target language. There are great dangers in this analogizing. The fact is, of course, that we do not control the learner as we do a computer: we do not control the input, we do not control the operations performed on the data, and we have only the sketchiest picture of what the output is. Furthermore the learner is not simply a data-processing machine, but also a learner. That is, the program is constantly being modified in response to feedback from the processing operation itself. If we must use data-processing terminology we must make a number of distinctions in our terminology. In one sense the teacher controls the data. It is in his hands to present or withhold potential input. It is not in his hands to ensure input. He has a number of techniques whose object is to ensure input, but his only means of checking whether input (or intake) has taken place is by making inferences from the linguistic performance of the learner. Furthermore, he has a number of techniques whose object is to control the processing by the learner of the input.

The teacher has nothing strictly comparable to a program which he can feed into the learner to determine the operations the learner must carry out on the data, although the syllabus is in one sense part of a program. In another sense the learner is pre-programmed to process the input in a particular way. It may well be that some of our teaching techniques interfere with the smooth running of the learner's program. It may also well be that the sequence of data presentation, the syllabus, does not correspond with the logical processing requirements of the learner: that some data is presented prematurely so that it cannot form part of the intake, or that it is not readily available when it is logically required.

Research into the process of learning would seem, therefore, to be most fruitful if we could discover as a first step the correlations between the nature of the data presented with the state of the learner's grammar. That is, of course, not the same as saying that we are concerned with relating *input* with *output*, since, as I have suggested, we do not control the input and we can only infer the nature of the output from the learner's linguistic performance.

We already control the nature of the data and its sequence of presentation (at least in a formal teaching situation). What we have at present is only a rather inadequate means for inferring the nature of the learner's grammar.

The system is a dynamic one. Since it is impossible to feed all the data into the learner at one time and leave him to process it, like digesting a heavy meal, there will be a theoretically infinite number of states of his grammar. Since we do not know the optimum sequence of feeding him the data, we need to make a regular series of checks on his grammar to see the effect that exposure to certain data has had on the state of his grammar. By this means we might eventually discover what the optimal logical sequencing of the data was. Alternatively, as I have suggested elsewhere, we might allow the learner to seek his own data rather than impose some arbitrary sequence of presentation upon him. Whichever procedure we adopt, we still need a means for describing successive states of his grammar. The situation is, of course, similar to the investigation of child language acquisition, a difference being that in the case of child language acquisition we have even less idea of what the nature of the potential input is.

What we need then, I suggest, are longitudinal studies of a learner's language, a set of descriptions of his successive 'états de dialecte'. By comparing these and logging the changes and then correlating these with the data of potential input we can make inferences about the learning process. The problem with which I am therefore here concerned is that of making such descriptions and indicating the techniques available to us for doing them. These are, I suggest, of two sorts: what are called in the language of applied linguistics *testing* and *error analysis*. I shall consider each of these in turn.

The stated objectives of tests are several. Achievement tests are designed to determine what has been learnt of a known syllabus; proficiency tests are intended to give a picture of the state of knowledge of a learner, unrelated to any particular course of teaching. Diagnostic tests have the more limited aim of identifying areas of the target language which are not yet mastered. Aptitude tests are, of course, rather different inasmuch as their objective is to measure the potential ability of the learner to acquire a second language. What distinguishes the actual form of the three first sorts of tests is not so much the testing techniques as the contents of the test. It is a matter rather of *sampling*. Where achievement is being measured the sampling is based upon some known body of data – a syllabus; where proficiency is being measured, it is the whole language which is the body of data on which the sample is based. The difference between diagnostic and proficiency tests lies not in the data which forms the basis of the sample but in the use made of the results of the test. For diagnosis it is the features of the language which the learner shows, by his performance in the test, that he has difficulty with which are the focus of interest, whereas for a measurement of proficiency, it is just as important to note what the learner does know as what he does not know.

Proficiency tests then might provide a source of data for the description of a learner's 'état de dialecte'. They suffer, however, from two serious defects in this respect. Firstly the amount of data available from a test is very restricted. The test is based on a sample and this sample, since it is not related to a particular syllabus must sample the 'language as a whole'. One need say nothing of the problem of what might be meant by the 'language as a whole' or on what principles a sample which is representative might be made. Clearly it will depend upon some theoretical model, either of language structure or language performance. Since the theory of sampling rests on the assumption that performance in a sample of tasks predicts the performance of all tasks, a proficiency test aims to give a quantitative measure of the learner's knowledge of the language as a whole and not a qualitative statement of the nature of his knowledge. It does not, therefore, provide the sort of data on which a description of the learner's 'état de dialecte' can be based. The second defect of proficiency tests is that they are constructed on the basis of the target language. They ask the question: does the learner know this or that category of the target language, can he perform this or that process in the target language? The questions are necessarily of a 'yes/no' sort. Proficiency tests are not devised to ask the question: *what* does the learner know, what language does he use, what are the categories and systems with which he is working? To know that the learner cannot perform some target language operation may be useful for teaching purposes, but for the purposes of a description of 'état de dialecte' we wish to know what similar or equivalent operations he does use. It is in the nature of objective tests that the test items admit of only two solutions – right or wrong. It is possible sometimes to make inferences from the wrong answers as to the nature of the learner's language, but that is not what the test is devised to reveal. This is not to say, however, that some experimental techniques might not be devised (and some have been) to reveal the sort of information we would seek.

There is here a whole new area of investigation into the learner's language by means of experimental or test methods still to be developed. Where tests can be regarded as an experimental approach to the study of the learner's language, error analysis can be called the clinical approach to the same problem. Here it is not the experimenter who is determining the sample of data but the learner. But because the emphasis in 'error analysis' has, till now, been almost wholly concerned with the practical objectives of planning remedial syllabuses and devising appropriate techniques of 'correction', it too has suffered from similar inadequacies as a technique for describing the learner's 'état de dialecte', as proficiency tests. It too has been predicated on the assumption that the learner is talking an inadequate version of the target language. It too has been target-language based and as the name of the technique 'error analysis' has implied, concentration has been on what the learner does not do right in terms of the grammar of the target language. The assumption is that the learner's grammatical and appropriate utterances are evidence that he is at least in part using the categories and systems of the target language correctly and appropriately.

So long as the objectives of 'error analysis' were strictly practical, in the sense I have suggested, there might have been some justification of these assumptions, although as I hope to show, I think they were mistaken. Anyone looking at the spontaneous utterances of a learner using his 'transitional dialect' for real communication purposes (by this I mean to exclude all exercises using language in the classroom) quickly realizes that the superficial well-formedness of individual utterances in terms of the criteria of the target language is no assurance that error is absent. The utterances of a learner can be roughly classified into three categories: *superficially deviant; superficially well-formed and appropriate in the context;* and *superficially well-formed but inappropriate.* By the latter I mean that such utterances cannot receive the interpretation that a superficially equivalent utterance would receive if spoken by a native speaker in that context. To put it briefly, what we are concerned with in 'error analysis' is discovering the degree to which the learner expresses his 'messages' by means of the categories and rules which the native speaker of the target language uses. This means that the category of utterances which I have called *well-formed and appropriate* is of no interest (i.e. does not form part of the data of 'error analysis') because they are simply taken as 'utterances in the target language'.

If, however, our objectives in undertaking 'error analysis' are to make a description of the 'état de dialecte' of the learner then the 'well-formed and appropriate' utterances are clearly an important part of our data. But there is an additional reason for this, and it applies, in fact, just as forcibly to 'error analysis' for practical purposes. A learner's utterance may be both well-formed and appropriate and yet erroneous; we can call such utterances 'right by chance'. There are two ways in which this can be understood. The utterance may have been learnt as a holophrase, that is, learnt as 'an idiom', when it is, in fact, in terms of the target language, generable by perfectly general rules. An example of this was provided by a learner who quite appropriately produced: *What are you doing tonight?* Examination of a greater body of his other utterances revealed that he nowhere else used the progressive form for future reference. And yet, of course, this sentence is in no sense idiomatic in English. Secondly grammatical and appropriate utterances may be produced by rules which are not those of the target language. There is plenty of evidence that this occurs. To give just one simple example: the learner of German who produced the correct noun phrases: *die guten Bücher, meine besten Freunde, diese jungen Leute* also produced the deviant noun phrases: *viele anderen Frauen; wenige schlechten Fehler; einige ungewöhnlichen Sitten.* From this one inferred that the learner did not yet know the rules for the endings of adjectives in the prehead position (i.e. strong and weak declension). He worked on the principle that the adjective was always inflected with the ending *-en* when preceded by a determiner (in the nominative plural). His rules were *not* these of the target language, but produced a fair number of superficially correct and appropriate forms *by chance.*

One is, therefore, led to the conclusion that 'error analysis' necessarily involves as part of its data fully acceptable utterances. If this is indeed the case then the name 'error analysis' becomes somewhat misleading, since one is forced into the position of saying that *all* the learner's utterances are potentially erroneous whatever their surface structure or appropriateness may be; or, and I prefer to express it this way, whatever the surface form or apparent appropriateness of a learner's utterances, none are utterances in the target language. In other words, he is not speaking the target language at any time, but a language of his own, a unique idiolect, which no doubt shares many features of the target language.

The consequence of this is that the term 'error analysis' is no longer useful since it is based on the assumption that *only* his superficially deviant and inappropriate utterances are utterances not in the target language. This is what I meant by saying that 'error analysis' has hitherto been 'target-language based'. Furthermore, it also means that the term 'error' is just as inappropriate when the object of the analysis is a practical one, as I have characterized it, as when it is the more theoretical one of describing the learner's 'état de dialecte'. The position which I am adopting here is clearly the same as that adopted in the study of child language acquisition. The whole corpus of the infant's or learner's output is relevant data for the description of his language systems at any point in his learning career. The well-formedness or appropriateness of his utterances in terms of the adult language is irrelevant.

We can now turn to the more intractable problem of describing the learner's 'état de dialecte'. We have seen that proficiency tests, as at present devised, are unlikely to provide the type of data on which such a description can be based, not only because of their fragmentary character, and their target-language based criteria, but because the status of the learner's responses as 'utterances in his dialect' is in doubt. They do not provide utterances in a situational context of the sort necessary for any descriptive work to begin. This is not to say that they are 'contextless' but that the context is not one of normal communication. The status of his responses as utterances in his dialect is impossible to establish.

The usual data for a language description are the acceptable utterances of a native speaker. We immediately run into problems here when faced with the contextualized utterances of a learner. Firstly, the learner is not a native speaker of his 'transitional' dialect; it is not his 'mother tongue'. There are, in fact, no *native* speakers of his dialect. We can disregard for the moment that there may be other learners whose educational history and native language may qualify them to be regarded as speakers of the same dialect. It is true, of course, that, *in this sense*, each individual speaks a unique idiolect of his native language. This fact is disregarded by linguists, since they do not normally need to characterize the speech of individuals, and need only work, for their purposes, with such abstractions as 'a language' or 'a dialect'. For the linguist's purposes the notion of 'acceptability' has sufficient content since it can be shown empirically that there are groups of people identifiable by other than linguistic criteria, who agree over a wide range of data about the grammaticality and appropriateness of sets of utterances in certain given contexts. But for the study of language learning, I have suggested that it is necessary to be able to characterize the language of individuals. In these circumstances the problem of acceptability takes on a new aspect. There is only one solution: that every utterance of the learner must be regarded as an acceptable utterance in his transitional dialect. This is, of course, empirically testable by requiring him to assent to his own acceptance of his utterance. (I am ignoring necessarily the sorts of mistakes that any speaker may make which are classed generally under the category of slips of the tongue. A learner speaking his transitional dialect is presumably as liable to such performance failures as any other speaker, indeed, probably more liable.)

Thus we come to the conclusion that the concept of un-grammaticality or deviance is not applicable to the learner. Everything he utters is by definition a grammatical utterance in his dialect. We have thus no problem similar to that which the linguist faces when undertaking the description of a language, that is to say, of determining what his data are. We have, of course, the purely practical problem of paucity of data on which to work. This paucity is occasioned by the relatively low output of the learner, by the fact that he is the sole informant and more particularly by the fact that his dialect is, we hope, unstable. These are all problems shared by those who study child language acquisition.

The linguistic description of a language is of the sentences of a language. We are thus, in describing the learner's 'état de dialecte', faced with the question of the relation between his utterances and the sentences of his dialect. Let us now consider this in the light of Lyons' (1972) three processes of *regularization, standardization,* and *de-contextualization.*

Regularization is the process of re-structuring an utterance in order to eliminate the sorts of results of the adventitious failures of performance already referred to under the heading of slips of the tongue. The problem here is a real one, and is related to the question of acceptability. Since the learner is the only informant, our ability to *regularize* his utterances is crucially dependent upon his co-operation. It is true that a whole class of performance failures and interferences can be recognized without reference to the formal features of the utterance, for example, coughs, sneezes, hesitations, stutterings, and so on. But the recognition of transposition, wrong orderings, substitutions of segments, can only be made by the learner himself. It is a practical problem in description that most work is done on written data where the learner is not available for consultation and self correction. In these circumstances surface deviations cannot be confidently and unequivocally assigned to performance failure or to features of the transitional dialect. We have no recourse to the linguist's own intuitions, though it should be said that many teachers become quite passable performers in their learners' dialect.

Standardization, the second stage of idealization, is that of restructuring the speaker's utterances to remove the systematic variation between utterances from different individuals due to personal and sociocultural factors. At least at this stage no problems arise since the learner is the sole speaker of his dialect. From a practical point of view it may be desirable to characterize the 'language' of a group of learners. In such cases the process of standardization or normalization may be necessary. For the purposes here being considered this does not arise.

It is at the crucial third stage, that of *de-contextualization*, that the most severe difficulties are felt, precisely because the learner *is* the only informant. Our ability to de-contextualize his utterances depends almost wholly on our ability to interpret the speaker's message or intentions. The fact that the linguist in this case is not a speaker of the learner's dialect makes the situation comparable to the problem of describing both the language of an infant or some unknown language. There are, however, certain advantages we possess. We can have recourse to the learner's mother tongue to establish the speaker's meaning. In this respect our task is much easier than that confronting those attempting to establish the sentences of the infant learner, and secondly, the learner's dialect, we assume and certainly hope, bears some strong resemblance to the target language. Otherwise the problem of contextualization follows the usual course of making inferences about the learner's rules derived from similar utterances produced under different contextual circumstances. This is no more than to say that we do not infer the nature of a learner's sentences on the basis of the surface structure of one particular utterance.

So long as the study of a learner's language is target-language based, however, there is always the tendency to normalize and de-contextualize in the direction of the target language, that is, to relate the learner's utterance not to the sentence of his dialect, but to the equivalent sentences of the target language. Thus, to give just one purely hypothetical example, if, in reply to the question: *Whose car are we going in?* the learner were to reply: *John, if he gets here in time*, the tendency would be to relate this to the equivalent target language sentence: *We are going in John's car if John gets here in time*, whereas a more extended study of the learner's dialect might well show that the learner's underlying sentence was: *We are going in the car of John, if John gets here in time*. A decision as to whether this is the most probable account will depend upon the evidence from other utterances of the learner, that is, whether he elsewhere expresses possession by means of the *possessive case* or by *of*, or by some other syntactic device.

I can now summarize my argument. In order to make progress in the methods and materials of teaching second languages we need to be able to relate the materials and procedures used by the teacher to changes in the knowledge of the learner. For this we need longitudinal studies of learners expressed in terms of sequential sets of description of their 'états de dialecte'. The data on which these descriptions may be based could be drawn from proficiency tests or from error analysis, respectively representing the experimental and clinical approaches. At the present time both these approaches are target-language based, in the sense that the test items are devised, and analysis of errors is made, in terms of the grammar of the target language. It is proposed that a description of the learner's 'état de dialecte' can be better achieved by a recognition that what he speaks is not an inadequate or incorrect form of the target language but a peculiar transitional idiolect, which should be approached in the same way as the language of an infant or some unknown language. Then concentration on his specifically ungrammatical or inappropriate utterances which is characteristic of what is called 'error analysis' will lead to a distorted picture of his grammar. In other words, the concepts of *error* and *acceptability* have as little utility in the study of the learner's language as they do in the study of the infant's.

4 The role of interpretation in the study of learners' errors

Studying the errors made by learners of a second language needs no justification. It is something which teachers have always done for purely practical reasons. Along with the results of tests and examinations, the errors that learners make are a major element in the *feedback* system of the process we call language teaching and learning. It is on the basis of the information the teacher gets from errors that he varies his teaching procedures and materials, the pace of the progress, and the amount of practice which he plans at any moment. For this reason it is important that the teacher should be able not only to detect and describe errors linguistically but also understand the psychological reasons for their occurrence. The diagnosis and treatment of errors is one of the fundamental skills of the teacher.

But the study of errors is also a fundamental part of applied linguistics. It provides a validation of the findings of contrastive linguistic studies. Bilingual comparison is based on the theory that it is the differences between the mother tongue and the second language which the learner has to learn. Contrastive studies are undertaken in order to discover and describe the differences. Error analysis confirms or disproves the predictions of the theory lying behind bilingual comparison. In this sense error analysis is an experimental technique for validating the theory of transfer.

But error analysis goes beyond this; it aims at telling us something about the psycholinguistic processes of language learning. We hope to be able to draw certain conclusions about the strategies adopted by the learner in the process of learning. In this sense, error analysis is part of the methodology of the psycholinguistic investigation of language learning. We may go even further: since infants learning their mother tongue have been shown to follow a similar course of development we may speculate that the learning of a second language may have some optimum course which represents the most economical route between the first and second language. Longitudinal studies of the second language learner similar to those of the infant learning his mother tongue could be undertaken. In such studies the errors he makes would be the most important source of information about his linguistic development, and could lead to some account of what I have elsewhere called his built-in syllabus.

These preliminary remarks are intended to show the central position that error analysis occupies in applied linguistic studies. All the more important then that we should develop better techniques for the *identification* and description of errors. The satisfactory explanation of errors, which is our final aim, is dependent upon an adequate description of errors.

Description of errors is a linguistic operation. Errors are described by the application of linguistic theory to the data of erroneous utterances produced by a learner or a group of learners. The more adequate the linguistic theory the better will be the linguistic description of errors. We have seen the same development in contrastive analysis, where surface grammatical theories have proved inadequate to predict the learners' difficulties. Theories incorporating a deep grammatical component have proved much more adequate. We look forward now to learning even more by using semantic based models.

Unfortunately the level of description of errors still most often used by teachers is superficial. Errors are still classified on a superficial basis as *errors of omission* where some element is omitted which should be present; *errors of addition* where some element is present which should not be there; *errors of selection* where the wrong item has been chosen in place of the right one; and *errors of ordering* where the elements presented are correct but wrongly sequenced. This superficial classification of errors is only a starting point for systematic analysis. It is only the evidence or *data* for an analysis. It is usual for teachers to go a bit further in their classification. They will usually state at what *linguistic level* the error has been committed. For example, the omission, addition, wrong selection, or ordering may be at a graphological level. These are errors of spelling; or it may be at a grammatical or lexico-semantic level. By applying this classification to errors we get a matrix for the categorization of errors of this sort:

	Graphological Phonological	Grammatical	Lexico-semantic
Omission			
Addition			
Selection			
Ordering			

But even this categorization is still insufficiently deep or systematic. The omission of an article where it is required or the addition of an article where it is not required are classified in this scheme as different sorts of errors, whereas it is explanatorily more useful to consider them both as evidence for an incomplete knowledge of the *system* of identification or specification. A more adequate classification, then, is in terms of systems, such as tense, number, mood, gender, case, and so on. Such a classification of error is more abstract and systematic. When a learner says:

I am waiting here since three o'clock.

we do not explain anything by saying he has made an error of *wrong selection* and *omission* by selecting the one word *am* in place of the two words *have been*. We say he has selected the wrong tense: non-perfective in place of perfective. He has not yet mastered the tense system of English.

For our present purposes, however, the important thing to note is that we *identify* or detect his error by comparing what he actually said with what he ought to have said to express what he intended to express. In other words, we compare his erroneous utterance with what a native speaker would have said to express that meaning. We identify errors by comparing original utterances with what I shall call *reconstructed* utterances, that is, correct utterances having the meaning intended by the learner. We can regard the reconstructed utterances as *translations* of the learner's utterances into the target language. Error analysis in this respect is like contrastive analysis. Our starting point is always *pairs of utterances* which are by definition *synonymous* in a particular context, i.e. translation equivalents.

We can see now how crucial interpretation is to the whole methodology of error analysis. The reconstructed sentence is based upon our interpretation of what the learner was trying to say, upon the meaning he was trying to express. The whole success of our description of errors hinges upon the correctness of our interpretation of the learner's intentions or meaning. The first question we have to ask, then, is: how do we arrive at this interpretation? There are two ways, depending upon whether we have access to the learner or not.

1   If he is present we can ask him to say what he intended in his mother tongue and then translate his utterance into the target language. This is what I should call an *authoritative* interpretation and it provides us with an *authoritative reconstruction* of his original (perhaps erroneous) utterance.

2   If the learner is not available for consultation, we have to attempt an interpretation of his utterance on the basis of its *form* and its linguistic and situational *context*. If the learner's utterance is formally erroneous, we may have difficulty in deciding what he intended to say even with reference to the context or the situation. The understanding of speech in our own mother tongue is basically a matter of prediction. Most of the time our predictions are correct. This is just as well, or communications would break down. But the fact remains that we can never be absolutely sure all the time that we have interpreted correctly what people say to us in our own language. If we are in doubt, of course, we can check up on our interpretation by asking them what they meant. But this is possible only in a face-to-face speech situation. Furthermore, we have to be aware in the first place that we have not properly understood them. It is surprising how often we accept our own interpretation of what someone has said to us and only find out later that we have misinterpreted their words.

If we cannot be absolutely certain of making a correct interpretation in our own language, how much less can we be sure when attempting to interpret the language of a learner. Interpretations made only on the basis of the *form* and *context* of the learner's utterance (including what we may, as teachers, know about him and his knowledge of the language), I shall call *plausible interpretations*, and the corresponding reconstructions, *plausible reconstructions*.

Of course, when dealing with the utterance of learners, even in their absence, we can have recourse to what we know of their mother tongue. The learner who wrote 'I want to know the English' was French. The face-value interpretation *I want to get to know the English people* was ruled out by the context; reference to French showed that the, here, incorrect use of the definite article was derived from its normal use in French before the names of languages. Thus, while the interpretation which was eventually placed upon this erroneous sentence, i.e.

I want to know English.

could be called a *plausible* reconstruction, it was made with a great deal of confidence. It is with the problem of plausible interpretations that I am concerned in this paper. Much the greatest part of all error analysis is concerned with written or recorded data. It is, therefore, of the highest importance from a methodological point of view that we understand the problems involved in making plausible interpretations. It is at this point useful, however, to recognize that although this is the case, written or recorded data fall into two classes – those which are the spontaneous expression of the ideas and intentions of the learner, that is what we call *free compositions*, and those which represent the learner's attempt to *reformulate* in one way or another the ideas and intentions of others. These are represented by such material as *translations, resumés, retelling of stories*, and *dictations*. It is clear that in the latter case we have available an account of what the learner is trying to express independent of the learner's own words. There are clearly certain advantages in the methodology of error analysis in working with such data, but we should bear in mind two disadvantages: (a) the learner may make errors both in interpretation of the original text *and* in expression of that interpretation. We may have some difficulty in deciding whether we are dealing with errors of understanding, reception, or errors of expression. (b) The sort of errors made will probably be differently distributed because of the likelihood of learners repeating holophrastically complete phrases or sentences from the original text, or perhaps providing an ill-remembered and distorted version of such phrases and sentences. Error analysis of these types of data will be unlikely to permit us to form a satisfactory picture of the learner's transitional dialect.

I have spoken so far as if it was an easy thing to recognize erroneous utterances; they exhibit omissions, additions, wrong selections, and ordering. However, a sentence may still be erroneous and show no outward and formal signs of this. It may be perfectly well-formed and yet be erroneous in the context. Purely superficial formal correctness is no guarantee of absence of error. A learner may produce a superficially well-formed sentence which, when interpreted according to the rules of the target language, does not mean what he intended to mean. This should not be a matter of surprise to anyone. Well-formed sentences produced by native speakers are mostly ambiguous when taken out of context. It is the context which enables us, mostly quite subconsciously, to place the intended interpretation on such ambiguous sentences.

Let us therefore look for a moment at this question of superficial well-formedness. Linguists are accustomed to speak of utterances as being *acceptable* or *unacceptable*. These are semi-technical terms. An acceptable utterance is one which could be produced by a native speaker in some appropriate situation and recognized by another native speaker as being a sentence of his language. Judgements about well-formedness, about ambiguity, and the ability to produce well-formed sentences are what is meant by the *competence* of a native speaker. This is what most linguistic theories are about. But you will notice the qualification I made '*produced by a native speaker in some appropriate situation*'. Performance ability in a language is not confined simply to competence, to the ability to produce well-formed sentences. It includes the ability to produce these sentences in the appropriate situation. We therefore have to consider not just the *acceptability* of sentences produced by a learner, but also their *appropriateness* – their proper relation to the context. If we consider well-formedness as a matter of the language code, then appropriateness has to do with the proper use of the code what linguists call *performance*. Judging the adequacy of performance is much more difficult than judging the adequacy of competence. Judgements about the appropriateness of an utterance require that we interpret it in relation to its context and the situation in which it is uttered. Appropriateness has many dimensions and cannot at the present be reduced to rules. Judgements about appropriateness must therefore be largely subjective. What is clear is that a well-formed acceptable utterance may be perfectly appropriate in one situation and not in another. An utterance like:

. . . and then the wolf said . . .

is appropriate in a fairytale-telling situation but inappropriate in any other. It might be difficult to find any context in which the utterance:

This elephant has fifteen legs.

was appropriate, and yet it is formally acceptable. But from the point of view of language teaching, at least in the earlier stages, we are unlikely to be called upon to judge this sort of appropriateness. There are, however, two fairly clear-cut dimensions of appropriateness which have relevance in error analysis. The first is what I shall call *referential appropriateness* and is judged by the *material truth value* of the utterance (in the logician's sense). If a learner says: 'I have a hat on my head' and we see that he is wearing a cap or that he is bare-headed, then we judge his utterance *acceptable* but *inappropriate*. His utterance was apparently well-formed according to the rules of formation of English, but situation/contextually misapplied. If he *writes*: 'I wore a hat to visit my aunt last week' then we can judge his utterance acceptable, but we cannot be sure of its appropriateness, since we do not know whether it is true or not. The examples I have given are fairly clear-cut, but this is by no means always the case. The learner who said: 'I am studying English' produced an acceptable sentence, but its appropriateness was difficult to judge since we reserve the term *study* in the cases of languages to people who have already achieved considerable competence and are studying in the university, for example. It is normally inappropriate for someone still at school to claim that he is *studying French*. The appropriate form would be *'learning French'*.

This is the problem which some linguists call the problem of *referential boundaries*. Certainly part of the learning of a language involves the learning to draw these boundaries in the way a native speaker does.

The second type of appropriateness which concerns us is *social appropriateness*. This is much more difficult to judge. It has to do with the selection of the appropriate style or register of language for the social situation. This is where 'Sprachgefühl' comes in, since we lack at the present time any adequate account of appropriateness of style and register. If a pupil greets his teacher with the words: 'Well, how are we today, old man?' his language is perfectly acceptable but socially inappropriate. There is no need to elaborate this point further here.

Sentences are erroneous therefore if they are unacceptable or inappropriate. A sentence may be *acceptable* and *appropriate*; or *unacceptable* but *appropriate*; or *acceptable* but *inappropriate*; or, of course, both *unacceptable* and *inappropriate*. Diagrammatically thus:

acceptable	appropriate	free from error
acceptable	inappropriate	erroneous
unacceptable	appropriate	erroneous
unacceptable	inappropriate	erroneous

We can see from this diagram that superficial well-formedness alone is not a guarantee of freedom from error. Only sentences which are both *acceptable* and *appropriate* may be error-free. However, we must enter one caution here. Just because a sentence is acceptable is no proof that the learner knows the rules by which it is formed. He may have learnt it parrot-fashion as a whole or as a formula, or he may have arrived at the correct form by the application of incorrect rules. A learner who can greet someone acceptably and appropriately with 'How do you do?' has not necessarily learnt the complicated rules for the use of *do* in the formation of interrogative sentences in English; he has learnt the sentence as a formula. But the learner of English who asked: 'What are you doing this evening?' produced both an acceptable and appropriate utterance. His teacher knew, however, that he did not yet know the use of the continuous present tense to refer to future plans. He had not yet learnt the rules for generating this sentence, but produced it by chance – he may have heard someone say it and learnt it as if it were an idiom or formula, which it is not. Learners then may be *right by chance*.

Superficial well-formedness is no guarantee of freedom from error. It is for this reason that we have to distinguish between sentences which are *overtly erroneous*, i.e. are superficially erroneous, and those which are *covertly erroneous*, i.e. apparently acceptable, but so by chance, or which are inappropriate in one way or another.

Judgements about superficial well-formedness, of course, do not need to take into account the context of the sentence; judgements about appropriateness, however, clearly do.

We can now return to the distinction between *plausible* and *authoritative* interpretation. When we can obtain an authoritative interpretation of a learner's utterance, there is usually no particular difficulty about deciding whether it is appropriate or not. Our only problem is deciding whether he produced the acceptable form *by chance* or *by design*. Only thorough familiarity with his knowledge of the language will enable us to decide. Where we have only plausible interpretations to work on, then our problems are much more complex. I shall devote the remainder of my discussion to them.

Let us take first of all those utterances of a learner which are *superficially well-formed*, i.e. acceptable. These may be, as we have seen, either *free from error* or *covertly erroneous*. Which we judge them to be will depend on our guess as to the meaning the learner intended to convey, that is our plausible interpretation. There are four possibilities:

1   He produces a well-formed sentence and we interpret it at its face value correctly. This is the normal situation, we presume, in conversation between native speakers. The only thing we have to take into account is, as we have seen, that he may have produced the correct sentence by chance.

2   The second possibility is that he produces a well-formed sentence and we interpret it at its face value but incorrectly, since the interpretation we give it appears to be appropriate. When the English learner wrote: *Ich brachte meine Freundin nach Hause* it only turned out later that the teacher realized that the learner intended to convey the meaning that he 'brought his girlfriend *to his own house*'. This is an interpretation which the German sentence cannot receive. An example from a German learner of English: *You mustn't wear a hat at the party*, where she intended: *You don't need to wear a hat* rather than *You must not wear a hat*. It may sometimes be difficult to detect errors of interpretation of this sort, since only an extended context can provide the information for the correct interpretation.

3 Thirdly a learner may produce an acceptable utterance which may, according to the rules of the language, receive two possible and equally likely interpretations in the context, only one of which represents what the learner intended. This situation is probably not very common and is one which may equally well happen among native speakers. An example: *I left behind the packet I bought in the shop*. Again only an extended context may resolve the ambiguity. As we shall see, ambiguity of interpretation is much more common where the original sentence is overtly erroneous.

4 The fourth possibility is that the sentence may be well-formed but totally uninterpretable in the context. The learner of English who wrote: *He gave, in contempt, an explanation of the situation*, produced a well-formed sentence, but one which, in the context, was totally uninterpretable. Not even a guess could be made at what the learner had intended to express by his use of *in contempt*.

So much for the interpretations of well-formed sentences. We can see that the second and fourth examples involve sentences which were *covertly* erroneous. We can now turn to the situation when the learner's sentence is *overtly* erroneous in one way or another.

5 The first case is when the erroneous sentence is interpreted correctly according to the learner's intentions. This is the most usual situation. It is fair to assume that we can make a correct plausible interpretation of the great majority of the erroneous sentences produced by learners, particularly if we are familiar with them and with their mother tongue. Thus, if we know that German learners very often use a non-perfective form with adverbial phrases of time with the preposition *since*, e.g. *I am waiting here since 3 o'clock*, then we will not be making faulty reconstructions if we interpret this as *I have been waiting here since 3 o'clock*. The only other possible but most unlikely interpretation would be something like: 'I am waiting here *until* 3 o'clock'. But the context would certainly show whether this was a possible interpretation or not. In other words, most overtly erroneous sentences are not ambiguous in their context.

6 The second possibility is that we place an incorrect interpretation on the erroneous sentence. This may happen more often than we realize. It is difficult to detect such errors of interpretation, precisely because, when we have found an interpretation which appropriately fits the context, we do not seek any further alternative interpretations which may be less probable. And yet as we well know, it is, in normal conversation, far from easy to predict what a person is going to say. The moral here is that we should not always be content with the first or most likely interpretation of an erroneous sentence. We should take a longer context into account in seeking for the learner's meaning.

7   A third and very common situation is one in which the overtly erroneous sentence is clearly ambiguous; in which it can be interpreted equally appropriately in either of two ways, in the context. The learner who wrote:

   A woman of her fifties

produced such an utterance. The two interpretations

   A woman of fifty
   A woman in her fifties

were, of course, both equally acceptable in context. Reference to the mother tongue may be of help in such cases.

8   Finally, we have the situation where the overtly erroneous sentence is so obscure that no interpretation of any sort, even taking into account the mother tongue, can be made. Such was the case with this utterance:

   If you want Indians very lovely, you will talk them.

The conclusion we can draw from this discussion is simple but far-reaching: namely, that the well-formedness or otherwise of a learner's utterance is not the only criterion for establishing the presence of errors, but that what is crucial is whether the normal target language interpretation of his utterance is appropriate or not in the context. The success of error analysis depends upon having adequate interpretations. Every utterance of a learner, whether well-formed or not, is potentially erroneous. Only a careful investigation of the meaning he intended to express will provide us with a means for determining whether an error is in fact present or not.

5 Error analysis and remedial teaching

It is now generally recognized that that branch of applied linguistic activity which is usually called *error analysis* has two functions. The first is a theoretical one and the second a practical one. The theoretical aspect of error analysis is part of the methodology of investigating the language learning process. In order to find out the nature of these psychological processes, we have to have a means of describing the learner's knowledge of the target language at any particular moment in his learning career in order to relate this knowledge to the teaching he has been receiving. The practical aspect of error analysis is its function in guiding the remedial action we must take to correct an unsatisfactory state of affairs for learner or teacher. It is with this second function of error analysis that I am concerned in this chapter. I want to investigate what role it plays in the specification and planning of remedial action. To do this we shall need to analyse in some detail the nature and cause of situations in which the need for remedial action seems to arise. This chapter will therefore fall into two parts – a discussion of what is meant by remedial teaching on the one hand, and the nature, scope, and problems of error analysis on the other. This will enable us to come to some general conclusions about the usefulness and limitations of error analysis in planning remedial courses.

In general we can say that remedial action becomes necessary when we detect a *mismatch* or disparity between the knowledge, skill, or ability of someone and the demands that are made on him by the situation he finds himself in. This general definition is true of all fields of human activity, not just language teaching and learning. It could almost serve as a definition of any learning situation. We reserve the term *remedial*, however, specifically for those situations which occur contrary to our plans and expectations, where the demands of the situation could not have been foreseen or, if foreseen, could not have been avoided – that is, where they lie outside the control of the language teaching planners, or the normal curriculum structure in an educational system.

In our ordinary experience of everyday life, if we, as individuals, foresee that some situation is going to make demands on us which we judge we do not have the knowledge or ability to meet, we avoid that situation; but there are many cases where the language learner has no choice; this may happen within the educational system or outside it – where, for example, a learner or a group of learners for whatever reason have not been able to benefit by the teaching they have received and are required to meet a new learning situation for which they are consequently unprepared. Or, for example, outside the school system where a learner or a group of learners are required to make use of their knowledge of the language in some task for which this knowledge is in some way inadequate, as frequently happens when students are required to use a foreign language in their university studies or in some professional occupation.

The problem which faces those responsible for decisions concerning remedial action is twofold. They must firstly decide whether, in any particular case, remedial treatment is called for and secondly, if it is called for, what the nature of such treatment should be. Let us take these two problems separately.

I suppose it is true to say that in many situations of language use there is some degree of mismatch between the knowledge possessed by someone and the demands of the situation. It is even true of native speakers. None of us possesses a complete and perfect knowledge of our own language. There are many situations which we avoid because we feel we are not equipped to cope linguistically with them. However, for the most part the mismatch is not so great that remedial treatment is necessary. This is true of many language learners in many situations – they will, as we might say, 'get by' in those situations with the knowledge they possess. This level of mismatch is what we would call an acceptable degree of mismatch and does not require remedial treatment.

The second level of mismatch is one in which the learner does not possess the necessary degree of knowledge to cope adequately with a situation, but has a sufficient basis of knowledge, together with such personality features as motivation and aptitude for learning, for him to be able to learn what is demanded by the situation with, or without, specific treatment. This is what we can call a remediable degree of mismatch. Whether we decide that formal remedial teaching is necessary or not in any particular case depends upon many factors – motivation, intelligence, and aptitude being one set of factors, the cost-effectiveness of remedial treatment being another. When well-motivated, intelligent, and apt students find themselves in such situations, many will adapt quite effectively without treatment. In other cases, if only in order to promote their self-confidence, remedial teaching may be useful.

The third level of mismatch is one in which the degree of

mismatch between knowledge and the demands of the situation is too great to be remedied economically. In such cases there is no solution but to remove the learner from the situation. This we can call an irremediable degree of mismatch. Such a situation occurs when a post-graduate student has been accepted for studies in the university where a near-native knowledge of the language is required and his knowledge falls far short of this standard.

Clearly, degrees of mismatch are infinitely variable in practice. The real problem facing those concerned with remedial teaching is to determine in any particular case the degree of mismatch that exists. And here we are up against a serious difficulty. How do we measure this? It is not unlike the problem of measuring the degrees of difference that exist between pairs of different languages when we are trying to predict the amount of learning that the speakers of one will have to do when trying to master the other. In such situations we attempt to do this by comparing the two languages systematically. In the attempt to assess the degree of mismatch we may use language tests – this is what is often done and such tests are said to be predictive, since their object is to predict how well a learner will cope with the new situation. Such tests are, however, *quantitative*, not *qualitative*, and as we shall see, most, if not all, language tests at the present time must take a restrictive view of what is meant by a 'knowledge of a language'. I shall return to this problem again. Most often the degree of mismatch is assessed empirically or pragmatically by waiting to see how well the learner in fact copes with the new situation; or by self-assessment, when the learner himself decides how effectively he will cope with the new situation. Such self-assessment is usually highly unreliable.

Once the need for remedial action has been established by one means or another, the problem of the nature of such action has to be solved. In other words, we have to decide what aspect of knowledge, skills, or ability the learner lacks in order to cope with the situation. Whereas a degree of mismatch is a quantitative assessment, the nature of mismatch is a *qualitative* assessment. We can call this a problem of diagnosis. This is essentially an applied linguistic problem, since it involves a study of the *nature* of the learner's knowledge of the language (not a measurement of the knowledge); it involves drawing a picture of what he knows and can do with what he knows. It requires some theoretical answer to the question: what do we mean by a 'knowledge of a language'? It is precisely at this point that, in my opinion, too many plans for remedial teaching fail, because they are based upon an inadequate model of a 'knowledge of a language' and often lead to merely repeating, or 're-teaching', what has already been taught and possibly even already learnt, instead of being based upon a careful study of the linguistic demands of the situation.

In order to discover the nature of the mismatch which requires treatment we have, then, not only to have some theoretical notion of what is meant by a 'knowledge of a language', but also of what is meant by 'the language of a situation'.

Up till recently the notion of 'the language of a situation' was understood in terms of such categories as style, register, medium, etc., but recent work in sociolinguistics has suggested that the attempt to describe 'the language of a situation', such as 'medical English' or 'legal English' as a sort of 'special language' like a dialect, in the sense of a 'special code' having its own syntactical peculiarities and its own vocabulary is, at best, only a partial explanation, and that the ability to communicate adequately in any situation involves more than the possession of a code. It is fundamentally a problem of knowing how to use a code, what has been called a knowledge of the 'speaking rules', since it is now becoming evident that there are rules for how to use the code and to interpret utterances in the code. This rather more extended concept of a 'knowledge of a language' has been called 'communicative competence'. That there is more to a 'knowledge of a language' than a knowledge of its structural rules, or of a code, is, of course, well known to teachers, who frequently meet students whose knowledge of the formal properties of the language seems to be rather restricted and who can nevertheless make use of what they know very effectively in quite a large number of everyday situations of language use, while there are other students who appear to have a good knowledge of the language code but nevertheless seem unable to use it effectively in the world outside the classroom. The 'language of a situation' then is more than a code; it is analysable in terms of the sort of functions language has in that situation – what language is used for in that situation. The analysis is in terms of such categories as speech acts or communicative functions. Unfortunately, analyses of this sort are still in a fairly preliminary stage. The sociolinguistic theoretical apparatus for analysis is still at a somewhat primitive level in comparison with that available for the analysis of language systems or codes, and, of course, what we cannot describe we cannot teach systematically. Learners may and do, however, learn much that we cannot teach them.

The decision, then, whether remedial treatment is necessary or not is a problem of the degree of mismatch between knowledge of the language and the demands of the situation, while the problem of the nature of the treatment depends on a study of what the learner knows and can do with his language and what the communicative demands of the situation are.

Remedial treatment can, in theory, be applied in two directions: bringing the learner's knowledge up to the standard required by the situation or bringing the demands of this situation into accord with the learner's abilities in the language. The first is the usual solution, but we cannot entirely neglect the second possibility. In most cases an opportunity to alter the situation favourably is not within our power. This is certainly true where the situation is controlled by demands of a non-linguistic sort. For example, we cannot imagine changing the fact that the language of aviation is English, or, even if we accept that, changing the level of knowledge of English that is required of airline pilots – our lives as air-travellers would be at risk! We may, nevertheless, be able to consider altering the situation within a school system where a too rigid curriculum is imposed by authority, one which takes too little account, for instance, of the considerable variability that exists in learners' motivation, intelligence, or aptitude. Where remedial treatment is found necessary in a school situation we can say that nearly always it is the system which is at fault and not the quality of the teaching or, least of all, the fault of the individual learner. Where remedial treatment is regularly required in an educational system then there is something wrong with the system, and it is the system which requires remedy, not the learner. This may mean adopting more realistic norms/standards given the particular sort of student we have, or promoting alternative norms/standards for some sub-group of the student population. The particular solution depends fundamentally on the numbers of students in the various sub-groups, or the ability distribution in the student population.

This leads me to my final point in the discussion of remedial teaching: the explanation of why it is necessary. Generally speaking, those responsible for planning such treatment are required to cope with the problem as it is rather than try to remedy the state of affairs by changing the system. As we have seen, in many cases the situation lies totally outside the power of the remedial teacher to influence. Such, for instance, is the case of students who require a certain degree of communicative competence to pursue higher studies at the university. We cannot expect university teachers to change their linguistic demands for the sake of a minority of students, or prescribe non-existent textbooks in the students' mother tongue in the place of those in English, for example. Nor can we expect the remedial teacher to require that the teaching in the school system shall be adapted to the communicative needs of any single group of learners – for example, that the ordinary school system should train English learners to cope with commercial or technical situations of language use. Problems of this sort are unavoidable precisely because the school language teaching curriculum must be imprecise and general in its objectives in terms of communicative competence. School language teaching curricula can rarely have specific communicative objectives. They will, perhaps inevitably though, train the learners for no particular situation of language use. It is for this reason (the impossibility of establishing clear objectives in most cases) that most language teaching in schools concentrates on teaching the 'code' (i.e. the language system) rather than the 'rules of use/speaking', on the grounds that whatever else a student requires in order to cope effectively with any situation of language use, he must have some 'basic' knowledge of the language code – what is often called, perhaps misleadingly, the 'common core' of the language. It is also for this reason, among others of a practical sort, that our measuring instruments (i.e. tests) can only measure adequately this rather restricted aspect of a 'knowledge of a language', and consequently why tests have a rather limited utility as predictors of performance in actual situations of language use. Now it is true that there are very few situations of language use in which it would be remotely possible to measure a learner's success in his use of the language. But one of these is that of students studying at the university in a language other than their mother tongue. To some degree, in such a situation, the communicative competence of a student in the foreign language must play a part in his academic success, though just how big it is as a factor may be impossible to determine. If such students' knowledge of the language code is measured by existing tests and then the results correlated with the students' results in academic examinations one might be able to find out what part a knowledge of the code (note: the code, not of the *use* of the code) played in the academic performance. Such an investigation has now been undertaken in the University of Edinburgh and it is encouraging to note that a significant correlation between students' knowledge of the code and their academic examination results has been found. This has meant that the language tests we use can be used to predict, although not very precisely, a student's academic success. But what is particularly relevant is that we can now identify fairly well on the basis of our test results which students do *not* require remedial treatment of their English, which can benefit by it, and which show what I have called earlier an *irremediable mismatch* between knowledge of the language and the demands of the situation. For these latter there is nothing to be done but to send them away from the university, since it is not regarded as part of the university's teaching function to provide full-time non-intensive language teaching courses in English. In other words, what they require is not remedial treatment at all, but a normal course in English.

We may note, however, that this testing programme in Edinburgh merely measures the *degree of mismatch* which I spoke about and which enables us to identify that sub-group of students requiring, and able to benefit from, remedial treatment, out of the total group of foreign students; it does not tell us what the nature of the remedial treatment should be. For that, as I have said, we need to know the *nature* of the mismatch. In the example given it requires a description of the demands of the academic learning situation in terms of communicative skills. I am glad to say that there are now several groups working on such an analysis. It also requires a technique for analysing the student's 'knowledge of the language', not just his 'knowledge of the code' (which is what our present tests can measure).

It is now time to turn to my second topic, that of error analysis. We do this in order to see to what extent and in what situations 'error analysis', as we can do it, may help us in assessing the student's 'knowledge of the language'. Error analysis is both an ancient activity and at the same time a comparatively new one. In its old sense it is simply the informal and often intuitive activity of any teacher who makes use of the utterances of his pupils to assess whether they have, or have not, learnt the particular linguistic points that he has been trying to teach – it is, in other words, an informal means of assessing and checking on a pupil's progress. Most teachers are perfectly well able to give an account of the typical errors made by the students who pass through their hands; they often build up a useful list of so-called common errors. Notice that this is almost always concerned with the student's knowledge of the code, and practically never with the student's communicative errors or failures. This is because, as we have already said, most classroom teaching still concentrates on teaching the code and not communicative competence, and because teachers are rarely in a position to observe their pupils' performance of the language in real situations of language use. In other words, most teachers simply do not know, from first-hand experience, how well their students will perform when they really have to use the language for communication. They can only guess. Certainly the ordinary tests and examination results will not tell them reliably. Teachers necessarily rely on this intuitive analysis of the students' knowledge to show them where the main learning problems of their students lie, and also to guide their informal in-course remedial work. This most often takes the form of 're-teaching' that particular bit of the language which has proved to be a problem – by re-teaching I mean simply teaching again by the same methods and with the same materials the point in question. In the event, very often, a lot of work produces relatively little improvement. After all, if the first teaching did not produce the required results, there is no obvious reason why the second teaching should do so (unless the first attempt was too hurried). Effective remedial teaching of this sort requires that we should *understand* the nature of the pupils' difficulties. In other words, it is not sufficient merely to classify his errors in some superficial way, as is too frequently done, into errors of commission, omission, wrong sequence, and wrong selection, but it requires a deeper analysis of the error, leading to an understanding or explanation of the cause of the error. Only when we know *why* an error has been produced can we set about correcting it in a systematic way. This is why 're-teaching' as a remedial procedure is so often unproductive. Inasmuch as the errors were a result of the method of teaching in the first place, there is no reason to hope that simple re-teaching will quickly solve the problem. If, on the other hand, the errors were a *natural* result of the learning process, such as *analogical errors*, or of the nature of the learner's mother tongue – *transfer errors* – then only a deeper understanding of the learning process on the one hand, or a linguistic comparison of the mother tongue and the target language on the other will yield explanations. This is where knowledge derived from linguistic and psycho-linguistic theory come in and why 'error analysis' is now increasingly engaging the interest of applied linguists. This is because, as I said in my introductory remarks, it yields insights into the language learning process which will eventually have direct relevance in the improvement of language teaching materials and methods, not only in remedial teaching but also in ordinary teaching.

This is the way the applied linguist sees the problem: a language learner is engaged in the task of discovering the system or code of the target language. He does this by making for himself, usually subconsciously, a set of hypotheses about how the language works on the basis of the language data which is available to him, that is, the examples of the language in their context. He makes use, of course, in constructing these hypotheses, of whatever information or explanations may be given him by the teacher or the textbook, including, most importantly, any information from the context or from translation, about how these examples of the language are to be understood or interpreted. Inevitably he will form false or provisional hypotheses, either because the data is insufficient to form correct hypotheses straight away, or because he receives misleading information about the language. (I do not mean that the teacher gives him false information, but rather, incomplete information, or ambiguous information, so that he may perhaps quite logically draw the wrong conclusions.) The hypotheses he forms are the basis on which his utterances in the language are produced. Inevitably some of these will be erroneous. The teacher makes it quite clear to him when this is so. The pupil then attempts to re-formulate his hypothesis in a more adequate form on a reconsideration of the old data or on the study of new data or explanations given by the teacher. The pupil then tries again. This time his utterances may be acceptable, or, once again, erroneous. He re-formulates his hypothesis if necessary. And so on. Each new hypothesis is, we hope, closer to the true facts of the target language.

We can see from this analysis that at every moment in a learner's career he has what we can call a 'grammar', that is, a set of rules for making sentences. The only thing is, of course, that the rules are not always those of the target language. He has what William Nemser has called an 'approximative system' (or others an *interlanguage*) at each moment in his learning career. The applied linguist's study of the learner's language is an attempt to characterize the 'approximative system' of a learner (or a set of learners) from the data of his utterances. The applied linguist is thus, through this study, attempting to describe 'the learner's language' at any particular moment. To do this, however, he has to take into account, of course, not just those utterances which are erroneous in terms of the grammar of the target language but the *whole* of the learner's output. The task is fundamentally the same as that of describing the language of the infant learning his mother tongue, or some other unknown language. It is by this means that we can draw up a picture of what, till now, I have called the learner's 'knowledge of the language'. It will be clear now that what this means is the 'model that the learner has of the target language'. The model is inaccurate in various respects, but the model is always complete, it is a working model, a system, a language system, a grammar, and can be used for producing utterances which can be used for communicative purposes, often quite effectively. Let us be quite clear about this. The learner's language at any point in his career is systematic and potentially functional. What the applied linguist's study of the learner's language cannot do, any more than conventional tests can do, is say anything reliable about how effectively the learner can use his system in situations of real language use. In other words, the applied linguist's study of 'learners' languages' tells us about their code; it does not yet tell us anything interesting about their knowledge of how to use the code. On the other hand, we have already seen that there may be some connection between a knowledge of a code and its successful use. The conclusion we can draw from this discussion is that, since we must teach the target language code, any technique which enables us to describe the learner's code at any particular point in his career will give us information of a detailed sort on which to base our remedial teaching if we consider it necessary. We do this by comparing the learner's code as we have found it with the standard description of the target language's code and identifying the differences. It is the account of the precise nature of these differences which gives us the information which enables us to 'correct' the language learner's errors in a systematic fashion in our remedial teaching.

Let me now summarize what I have said. Remedial teaching is adjudged necessary when we discover a mismatch between a learner's (or group of learners') 'knowledge of the language' and the linguistic demands of some situation in which he finds himself. This situation may be *a situation of language learning*, as we may find it within a school system, or it may be *a situation of language use*, where the learner will have to use what he knows for real communicative purposes. The *degree of mismatch* determines whether and how much remedial teaching is necessary and is normally measured by language tests. We have seen, however, that these tests only measure the degree of mismatch in terms of a knowledge of the language code which is itself only part of the knowledge required to use language functionally in a situation of language use. It may, however, be the principal type of knowledge needed to cope with a situation of language learning.

The nature of this mismatch determines the nature of the remedial treatment. This cannot adequately be discovered by language tests, but requires an analysis of the situation of language use not only in terms of the nature of the language code used, but also in terms of the types of discourse functions it involves. A parallel assessment of the learner's code by means of 'error analysis' tells us the nature of the differences between the learner's code and that of the situation, and provides us with the information on which we may base a systematic remedial course. Error analysis, however, cannot yet give us a clear and comprehensive picture of the learner's communicative competence; it does not enable us to predict how a particular learner will cope with the demands of a situation of language use, though it will serve well to say how he will perform in a situation of language learning, as I have defined it.

Let me say finally that the study of the learner's language requires a good knowledge of linguistics to perform and is, thus, at present not a technique available to most present-day teachers. We have not yet even started, for lack of both theory and methodology, to study a learner's communicative competence. Until we can, the design of remedial programmes will remain, as it is at present, very much an art, and dependent upon the experience, skill, and ingenuity of the language teacher.

Note

Paper presented at the first overseas conference of the International Association of Teachers of English as a Foreign Language held in Budapest in 1974.

6 The elicitation of interlanguage

The use of the term 'interlanguage' in the title of this paper presupposes that the language learner at all points of his learning career 'has a language', in the sense that his behaviour is rule governed and therefore, in principle, describable in linguistic terms. That his language is changing all the time, that his rules are constantly undergoing revision is, of course, true and merely complicates the problem of description but does not invalidate the concept of 'a learner's language'. The study of the learner's utterances, by what is misleadingly called 'error analysis' tends to confirm this picture. His language behaviour is consistent in certain respects at a given point in his development but inconsistent in others. The fact that his language is impoverished or deficient as a means of communication is obvious. This is only what one would expect of someone developing a new way of doing something familiar.

If we approach the study of the learner's language as we would any unknown or undescribed language, then we must regard the learner as a 'native speaker' of his language and theoretically, at least, the *only* native speaker. We must attempt to describe his language in its own terms, at least in the first instance, and not in those of any other language. If what we are describing, following Chomsky, is his grammatical competence (or his transitional competence as I have called it elsewhere) then we must also accept that he will have 'intuitions' about the grammaticality of his language which are potentially investigable. The fact that he himself may regard them as intuitions about the target language is neither here nor there. In practice, of course, because of the paucity of data produced by an individual learner, we normally take our data from a group of learners which we treat as 'homogeneous', in just the same way as a linguist describes the competence of the 'ideal native speaker in a homogeneous society', 'idealizing' our individual variation. Now, if we adopt this approach, which I suggest is the appropriate one for research into language learning, then clearly, by definition, the learner, as a native speaker of his own idiosyncratic dialect, produces no errors, though like any speaker he may produce 'slips of the tongue or pen'. When we talk about *errors* made by learners we are clearly applying to their language intuitions about grammaticality possessed by speakers of the target language. What we are saying is that the learner is not yet a speaker of that language. This is like saying that a French speaker speaks erroneous English or, to make the analogy clearer, that the West Indian Creole speaker speaks erroneous standard English. There might seem to be good practical reasons for adopting this approach; the learner, after all, is meant to be acquiring the rules of the target language (the Creole speaker is not meant to be trying to speak standard English) and we want to identify the differences between the two sets of rules and discover what he has still to learn, so that we may take appropriate and remedial action, and, in a more general way, identify the principal learning tasks of a given group of learners in order to incorporate this knowledge in the devising of our syllabuses and teaching materials. Error analysis viewed in this way is a branch of applied comparative linguistics (contrastive linguistics, as it is unfortunately usually called).

But if we look at this matter a bit closer we shall see that it does not, in fact, resolve our problems. We now know that contrastive analysis cannot satisfactorily be pursued by imposing the descriptive framework of one language on the data of another, but requires the setting up of a common descriptive framework, a set of categories and relations common to both languages and 'neutral' as to the 'direction' of the comparison.

I want to suggest therefore that there is no methodological difference between error analysis and the study of the learner's language. The difference, if there is indeed one, lies rather between what is being compared. In *error analysis* we are comparing the learner's language with the 'whole' of the target language – or, more exactly, with what has been selected for incorporation in the syllabus, whereas in the theoretical study into language learning we are interested in the relation of what has been taught *so far* with the learner's knowledge at that same point. The first, then, is a *prospective* comparison and the other a *retrospective* comparison.

Let me expand this idea. If we regard the learner as a learning device, then, since we cannot study the device *directly*, by taking it to pieces, we have to *infer* its nature from a comparison of the *input to* the device with the *output from* the device, that is, the relation between the syllabus taught and the learner's grammatical competence at any particular point. (Notice that throughout this paper I am restricting myself to consideration of acquiring grammatical competence. This is largely because of our imperfect understanding of communicative competence.)

If there is not a one-to-one relation between input and output, and there obviously is not, then this tells us something about the nature of the device. It tells us possibly that we may have to make a systematic distinction between the notion of *input* and the notion of *intake*. The fact is that learners do not immediately learn, on first exposure, what the syllabus prescribes should be learnt at that point. There are two possible reasons for this:

1   that the nature of the data or the manner in which they are presented is defective in some way, which makes it impossible for the learner to take them in, or

2   while the data are adequate, the state of the learning device is such that it cannot take them in. In other words, the learner has to know certain things before he can learn something new. If we then attempt to teach him something before he is ready for it, the result will be confusion, false hypotheses, and what we could call redundant 'errors'. It appears likely that learners are programmed cognitively to process data in a certain way and the teacher is not in control of the program, although he has a number of techniques which aim at controlling the learning process. It may be that some of these techniques interfere with the smooth running of the learner's program. It may also be that the order in which the data is presented does not correspond with the logical requirements of the learner. Some data may be presented prematurely so that they cannot form part of the *intake*, or alternatively some data may not be available when they are logically required. It is clearly one of the main tasks in the research into the process of learning a second language to discover the relationship between the nature of the data presented and the state of the learner's grammar.

The learning system is a dynamic one; it is a process of interaction between the learner and the data provided – teacher and materials. Since we do not know the optimum sequence for presenting the data, we need to make a regular series of checks on the learner's grammar in order to discover what effect the exposure of certain data has had on the state of his grammar. By this means we might eventually discover what the optimum logical sequencing of the data was for any particular learner or group of learners. It is necessary to make this qualification since clearly what the learner already knows of a language (his mother tongue and any other languages he has) is part of the learning device itself. What we need then is a longitudinal study of learners exposed to particular syllabuses (captive learners), or even exposed to no particular syllabus (non-captive learners). The latter would resemble an investigation of child language acquisition. The difference being that in the latter case we have little idea at present of what the nature of the potential input to the device is. This, then, is the descriptive problem we face; what about the data with which we have to work?

When the linguist sets about describing an unknown language, he makes use of two sorts of data: what I shall call *textual data* and *intuitional data*. These are related to the two levels of adequacy, observational and descriptive. A description based only on textual data cannot achieve more than observational adequacy. As we know, there are an indefinite number of observationally adequate grammars possible of a textual corpus. To be descriptively adequate a grammar must accord with the intuitions of the native speaker. Error analysis is based on textual data and can therefore not achieve, in theory at least, more than observational adequacy. In practice, however, it is usually carried out by a teacher who has considerable insights into the linguistic development of his pupils and is usually bilingual in the mother tongue of his pupils and in the target language. He has therefore at some point in his career actually been a native speaker of his pupil's interlanguage. He is therefore usually in a similar position to the linguist when he is describing his own mother tongue who consciously or unconsciously makes use of his native intuitions about it. For this reason most error analysis implicitly incorporates considerable intuitional data. Most teachers can predict fairly well what their pupils will regard as acceptable or unacceptable forms, what they will regard as good paraphrases and what sentences they will understand as being related in one way or another. We can see this from the considerable confidence with which error analysts assign interpretations to the utterances of their pupils, although as we know a fair proportion of these, whether superficially well formed in the terms of the target language grammar or not, are potentially ambiguous. The analyst frequently simply overlooks this ambiguity because of the insights he has into his pupils' language.

Nevertheless, as we know, even linguistically sophisticated native speakers' intuitions about their language are not always readily available. We need therefore in the investigation of the learner's language to supplement *textual* data by *intuitional* data and devise systematic methods of investigating these.

There is a further reason for this. Textual data cannot be regarded as a representative sample of the learner's language. Quite apart from the paucity of textual data, to which I have already referred, the sample is biased. This happens in two ways: by external constraint and internal constraint. By this I mean that the textual data we usually work on is not spontaneous language produced by the learner under the pressure of natural communicative needs, but material produced as exercises in classroom conditions with a consequent variety of artificial constraints imposed on it – restricted topics, restricted functions, restricted time, etc., e.g. free composition, guided composition, retold stories, etc.

Secondly, the learner himself will place limitations upon the data we work with, by selecting from his actual repertoire, where possible, only those aspects of his knowledge which, rightly or wrongly, he has most confidence in. What we are using as a sample, then, is what the task selects and what the learner chooses to show us. Except in situations of real communicative need (rare enough in formal teaching situations) the learner will play safe. He will not reveal his hand.

We need, therefore, techniques which allow us to correct this sampling bias, which will enable us to elicit information about the learner's interlanguage which he is not required to reveal by the ordinary tasks we set him or which he does not care to reveal to us voluntarily. We have to 'put him on the spot'.

It might be thought that this is the function of tests and examinations. But this is not so. Essay type examinations of the traditional sort leave the learner free to choose his own language and are therefore no more revealing than ordinary exercise material, and tests are normally designed to measure what the learner knows of the target language, or, at least, that part of it he has been taught. The principal defect of tests is that they ask the wrong question from our point of view: does the learner know this or that category of the target language? Can he perform this or that process in the target language? The questions for reasons of objectivity and statistical processing are of a 'yes/no' type. Tests are not devised to ask the question: what does the learner know? What are the rules he is using and the systems and categories he is working with? To know that the learner can or cannot perform some target language operation may be useful for assessment, selection, or placement, but for descriptive purposes we wish to know what actual rules he uses. We may sometimes, of course, incidentally, be able to infer from the test results something about his system, but that is not what the tests are devised to reveal. The reason for this is that the format of tests requires the testee to select the correct target language response from a number of incorrect forms or 'distractors'. Now, it depends crucially on the nature of the distractors whether we can infer something about the nature of the learner's language from them or not. If the distractors are selected on the basis of a study of the sort of errors made by learners at the stage for which the test has been devised, then the way the testee responds may reveal something about his intuitions, but there is no reason in theory why test constructors should base their distractors on learners' errors, if their objective is simply to find out whether the learner can recognize a correct form or not. Furthermore if the test is intended for use by learners with different mother tongues then they cannot be based upon learners' errors anyway. Distractors can, after all, be invented purely on the basis of the description of the target language; they do not have to be selected from the learners' repertoire, though they often are. It is not impossible to imagine a test item in which the learner would wish to reject all the preferred alternatives, correct or incorrect, if he was allowed to, because none of them were generable by the grammar of his interlanguage, just as infants have been found to reject adult forms offered for imitation because their grammar would not generate them.

Though elicitation procedures may take the form of tests, they do not have to, nor, of course, are any statistical procedures involved, unless we want to make some general statement about the language of a group of learners. An elicitation procedure is any procedure which causes a learner to make a judgement about the grammatical acceptability of a form or provokes him into generating a linguistic response. It is clear that his judgements and responses can only be based upon the grammar of his interlanguage. To suggest otherwise is to suggest that a learner might say: 'That is the form a native speaker would use, but I use this form instead'.

Elicitation procedures are used to find out something specific about the learner's language, not just to get him to talk freely. To do this, constraints must be placed on the learner so that he is forced to make choices within a severely restricted area of his phonological, lexical, or syntactic competence. These constraints can be applied in two ways; as in ordinary tests, by limiting the range of possible choices, as in a closed item recognition test, or by restricting contextually the range of possible free choices as in an open-ended production test. But, and this is one of the principal differences between tests and elicitation procedures, the range and nature of the choices or judgements, and the selection of the contexts is based not upon a description of the target language, but upon what is known (however limited) of the learner's interlanguage. Thus for example the choices in a recognition procedure will be based upon what learners at that stage are known, believed, or may be predicted to do. The contexts for productive elicitation exercises will be selected to elicit lexical items or syntactic forms which learners have already produced or may be predicted to produce in such contexts.

It is clear therefore that for elicitation procedures actually to elicit the information sought by the investigator, the latter must have some prior hunch or hypothesis about the possible nature of the learner's interlanguage as a guide, otherwise he will simply be 'shooting in the dark'.

Where does the investigator get these hunches from? If he is the teacher of the learners in question, he will, from experience, have plenty of such notions. I have already suggested that he is, or was, a 'speaker' of his pupils' interlanguage (though he may reject the notion indignantly), but unless he is linguistically trained, these hunches will be unsystematic or unsystematizable by him. He must in addition have a general model of language structure within which to work in order to systematize his special knowledge and intuitions.

But the main, and linguistically most specific, notions about the learner's language will derive from the two systematic techniques already mentioned: formal error analysis and contrastive analysis. These are complementary. The role of contrastive analysis is now increasingly seen as explanatory rather than predictive. We now rely largely on contrastive analysis to explain the learner's language, though, of course, there are other explanations than language transfer.

As we saw, in theory, analysis of a textual corpus can yield no more than a number of merely observationally adequate accounts, that is, a number of equally likely hypotheses about what is going on. The selection of the most likely hypothesis, that is, the descriptively most adequate account, is the function of contrastive analysis. This is why, logically, the devising of systematic elicitation procedures must follow, not precede, as complete an explanatory study of the learner's language as the available data permits. Only when the data is deficient (as it nearly always is) are we forced to fall back on the predictive role of contrastive analyses.

As I see it then, we have a logical sequence of procedures in the investigation of the learner's language. Firstly, by a study of his textual output, supplemented by the hunches of teaching experience, where possible, we set up partial and tentative hypotheses about the learner's grammar, the most probably correct one of which is selected on the basis of a comparison of the mother tongue and the target language. This yields a set of specific hypotheses about the nature of the learner's language which are then submitted to experimental validation or refutation by means of a set of elicitation procedures.

I now want to look at some of these procedures more closely. There is, of course, nothing new in the idea of eliciting data from informants. It has always formed part of the methodology of descriptive linguistic research, as when the linguist has worked with what he called *native informants* of the language under description. We can borrow, in our own application, many of these techniques. We may also care to study the elicitation techniques of those studying child language acquisition. But there are a number of ways in which these three investigations are differentially constrained, which depend upon the knowledge and sophistication of the subject being investigated. The first requirement of an informant, or subject, in elicitation procedures is that he should be able to make judgements about the acceptability of forms submitted to him; he should also be able to make judgements about synonymy, contradiction, entailment, and other relations between the sentences submitted to him. This the second language learner and native informant can do, but the infant cannot, at least not directly (those studying child language have therefore to devise indirect means for eliciting such judgements). Secondly, in order to get at an authoritative interpretation of a linguistic form, the ability to give a translation equivalent is necessary (unless we depend upon non-linguistic behavioural evidence). This the second language learner can provide since he is, by definition, a native speaker of both languages. But a native informant may or may not be able to do so, depending on whether he is a full bilingual or not. Thirdly, in order to understand the instructions given in elicitation exercises some linguistic metalanguage is almost inevitably needed. But more importantly a metalanguage is needed for reporting the subject's introspection or intuitions about the nature of his language, its categories and systems. Most second language learners acquire such a metalanguage as a by-product of language teaching. This is clearly not the case with the infant. The native speaker informant may or may not have such a metalanguage. In the case of the study of obscure languages spoken only by people without formal education they will not.

We can summarize these different situations thus:

	Judgements of acceptability	Authoritative interpretations	Metalinguistic explanations
Infant	—	—	—
Native informant	+	(+) —	(+) —
Language learner	+	+	(−) +

From this analysis we can see that the investigator of the learner's language is in a relatively favourable position for the use of elicitation procedures. His informant is, by definition, a full bilingual, is capable of communicating his judgements about acceptability and usually is sophisticated enough to report in some metalanguage his intuitions about his interlanguage.

I shall now conclude by summarizing my arguments. To discover something about the processes of second language learning we need to be able to make longitudinal studies of language learners, correlating their linguistic development with the data which is put before them. This means making successive descriptions of their interlanguage. The data on which we base these descriptions is, in the first instance, a body of utterances by the learner – the *textual data*. This is, however, both too small in quantity and, because of the internal and external constraints on its production, probably not a representative sample of the learner's language. It provides, however, when analysed, useful hypotheses about the nature of the learner's language. These hypotheses require explanatory refine-ment by contrastive analysis, and are finally validated or otherwise by elicitation procedures whose object is to gain access to the learner's intuitions about his language – *intuitional data*. The language learner appears to be a particularly favourable subject for such experiments by comparison with an infant or a native informant of some unknown language.

7 The study of interlanguage

In the course of learning a second language, learners will produce utterances which are ungrammatical or otherwise ill-formed, when judged by the generally accepted rules of the language they are learning. This is, of course, obvious not only to teachers of languages but to any native speaker of the target language who comes in contact with them. It is generally socially unacceptable to correct the errors of a foreigner speaking what he regards as our language unless we have been specifically asked to do so by him. It is however one of the most important tasks of the teacher in the language classroom, and it is part of the skilled technique of the teacher to decide when correction is necessary and to do it in a way that helps the learner to acquire most expeditiously the correct forms of the target language.

There are a number of ways in which teachers have regarded, and still do regard, the errors made by learners. They may consider them as being an unfortunate but inevitable sign of human fallibility – for example, lack of attention or poor memory on the part of the learner, or, if they are modest enough, some inadequacy in their own teaching. In such a case they will be dealt with by re-teaching the point in question, using the same teaching procedures and materials as were used initially. In other words, errors arise because there has not been enough effort on the part of the learner or enough explanation or practice on the part of the teacher. But either way there is no point in attempting to analyse the nature of the error, since greater and repeated efforts will correct it. It is just a random event, and if teaching and learning were maximally efficient, errors would not occur.

Another attitude to errors is that they are all the result of the influence of the mother tongue on the learning process, 'interference' as it was called, from the habits of the first language. The undoubted similarity of certain forms produced by many learners in their attempts to write and speak the target language to those of their mother tongue led to a whole industry dedicated to the investigation of the similarities and differences between languages, so that the errors of learners might not so much be explained when they occurred, as predicted before they occurred, and thus, by suitable techniques of teaching, be prevented perhaps from occurring. But learners still went on making errors and many of them were now recognized not to have any clear relation to the features of the mother tongue. So an alternative way of looking at them is now to be found. They are regarded as useful evidence of how the learner is setting about the task of learning, what 'sense' he is making of the target language data to which he is exposed and being required to respond. The making of errors, in this approach, is seen as an inevitable, indeed a necessary part of the learning process. By studying them the teacher may gain insight into the learner's state of knowledge at any particular moment and also into the strategies of learning that the learner may be using. With this understanding he will be in a better position to devise appropriate corrective measures. This latter approach, however, clearly assumes that learners' errors are in some sense systematic and not random, otherwise there would be nothing for the teacher to learn from them. But, if the learner's errors are systematic, then his own peculiar version of the target language must be based on some systematic knowledge or personal 'competence', to use Chomsky's term; in other words he must possess a more or less well-defined personal grammar to base his utterances on. If that is the case, we can talk about his performance as being rule-governed in the same way as we speak of the performance of any native speaker of a language as rule-governed. Now even the most cursory study of the utterances of learners at any particular stage in the course of learning a second language shows that their errors are to a considerable degree regular and consistent. Indeed experienced teachers are able to predict rather accurately *what* errors any specific group of learners is going to make in the next stage of the course, however hard they may try to prevent these occurring. Inasmuch as the learner's verbal performance in the second language is structurally systematic, we are entitled to speak of him at any particular point in his learning career as possessing a 'language', idiosyncratic though it may be. These learners' versions of target languages were given the collective name *interlanguage* by Selinker in 1972, and it is this term which has gained the widest currency among applied linguists in recent years.

The study of interlanguage is, then, the study of the language systems of language learners, or simply the *study of language learners' language*. Other names for learners' language have been proposed. James coined the term *interlingua* and Nemser offered *approximative systems*. I myself have written about the learner's *transitional competence*. Each of these terms draws attention to different aspects of the phenomenon. The terms *interlanguage* and *interlingua* suggest that the learner's language will show systematic features both of the target language and of other languages he may know, most obviously of his mother tongue. In other words his system is a mixed or intermediate one. This emphasizes one dimension of variability in the language of language learners. The term *approximative system*, on the other hand, stresses the goal-directed development of the learner's language towards the target language system. My own term *transitional competence* borrows the notion of 'competence' from Chomsky and emphasizes that the learner possesses a certain body of knowledge which we hope is constantly developing, which underlies the utterances he makes and which it is the task of the applied linguist to investigate.

The phenomenon of human language, the structural properties of which it is the aim of theoretical linguistics to explain, is realized in a myriad variety of concrete forms, typically, in the awareness of most people, in the various socially institutionalized, described, and named language systems to be found in the world. A language is thus a *particular* manifestation of the phenomenon of human language. By describing and comparing these different manifesta tions, the linguist attempts to find out what are the 'basic' properties of all human language; he seeks for universals. Similarly the phenomenon of interlanguage manifests itself in a variety of forms. But while linguistics has traditionally concerned itself with the institutionalized realizations of human language – that is with 'langues' in de Saussure's terminology, rather than with the particular idiosyncratic manifestations of the individual native speaker's versions of particular languages, that is with *idiolects* – or 'parole', in one interpretation of this term in de Saussure's usage – this has not been the case, anyway until recently, in the study of the phenomenon of interlanguage. The reasons for this are fairly clear. Until we have overcome the theoretical and methodological problems of describing the approximative systems, or idiosyncratic grammars, of *individual* learners, or possibly groups of learners, we are not in a position to make firm generalizations about the phenomenon of interlanguage. Interlanguages, in any case, are not socially institutionalized forms of behaviour (except perhaps in rare cases) and consequently we do not have names for 'approximative systems'. We cannot, in other words, use the de Saussurean framework as a starting point for our study. The effect of institutionalization is to establish accepted norms of behaviour in a language community and thereby keep within certain bounds the variability of individual idiolects. This is clearly necessary if a language is to serve as a means of communication within a society.

But interlanguages are rarely used for regular communication between their speakers. They are not institutionalized manifestations of language. They do not therefore develop 'norms'. Indeed the norms which interlanguage speakers implicitly accept and aim at are those of the target language. Approximative interlanguage systems are therefore unstable. It is because of the dynamic nature of approximative systems that their investigation presents peculiar theoretical and methodological problems not unsimilar to those found in the study of child language acquisition.

The principal theoretical problem is that linguistic theory has traditionally been developed for the description of stable, institutionalized, and therefore relatively well-defined manifestations of language. It is true of course that language systems do change over time, but change is relatively slow by comparison with the speed of change found in the developing language systems of the infant or of the second language learner. Linguistic theory copes with the problem of describing change by postulating a succession of 'stable states' or 'états de langue'. This simplifying assumption may have small consequence when dealing with the problem of slow change, but leads to peculiar problems when applied to processes of rapid change. The data in these circumstances will typically show a degree of inconsistency or lack of regularity not found in the data the linguist normally deals with. For this reason there have been investigators who have questioned the appropriateness of the term 'systematic' as applied to interlanguage phenomena. I suggest that much of the apparent inconsistency is an artefact of the theoretical models we are forced to use to describe the data. In other words, the learner's approximative systems merge gradually into each other rather than switch from one discrete state to the next.

This theoretical difficulty has been compounded by the methodological difficulty of collecting data. A language learner, at least in a formal instructional setting, does not in fact spontaneously produce much data for the investigator to work on. To a lesser extent this is also true of the infant whose language we may be trying to study. But unlike the data from infants' speech, that produced by learners derives from rather restricted and specialized situations of language use; learners do not use their interlanguage very often in the classroom for what we may call 'normal' or 'authentic' communicative purposes. The greater part of interlanguage data in the classroom is produced as a result of formal exercises and bears the same relation to the spontaneous communicative use of language as the practising of tennis strokes does to playing tennis. Indeed what goes on in the classroom in the target language can scarcely be called 'language use' at all. There is good reason to suppose that the interlanguage data generated in this sort of specialized verbal activity in the classroom does not offer us a representative sample of material on which to base an adequate account of the learner's knowledge at any particular stage of his career. Learners typically produce a different set of errors in their spontaneously generated utterances, when attempting to communicate, than in their practice utterances. They appear to operate according to two differing sets of rules. Widdowson refers to these as 'rules of use' and 'rules of usage' respectively. It is for this reason that we must take into account the utterances of learners when actively communicating. But this, alas, happens all too rarely in the classroom. This is why, in recent years, two tendencies can be observed. On the one hand there has been an increased interest in the study of learners in informal settings of language learning and use and, on the other, in the devising of techniques for getting at the learner's knowledge more directly than by inference from his functionally constrained utterances in the classroom. These techniques take the form of elicitation procedures of various sorts. They have the objective of requiring the learner to reveal what he knows, that is, his 'transitional competence' or 'approximative system' by responding to various types of tests. These procedures are, of course, different in form and intention from tests devised to *measure* the learner's knowledge of the target language system. Their objective is descriptive not evaluative.

Elicitation is a technique familiar to the linguist working with native speaking informants in the field and takes two forms: getting the informant to produce data of any sort or to produce data incorporating particular features in which the linguist is interested at that moment. The first type of elicitation is used where the investigator has not yet any well-formed hypothesis about the nature of the language he is investigating and merely requires raw data on which to make a start. The second type of elicitation is a closely-controlled procedure. Here the linguist already has some preliminary hypothesis about the language system he is describing and wishes to test it. In the study of interlanguage, the first type of investigation corresponds to what is often called 'error analysis' and is performed on any data elicited from the learner in, or outside, the classroom. On the basis of this preliminary analysis the investigator sets up specific hypotheses about the possible nature of the learner's approximative system, which he then attempts to test by means of controlled elicitation procedures.

These two methods of investigation we can call *clinical* and *experimental* respectively and they form the basic techniques used by any linguist investigating particular manifestations of language – child language, interlanguage, or institutionalized language. The degree to which experimental elicitation techniques may be used will differ in each case. It is not easy to use them with infants, since they involve the intelligent understanding and cooperation of the subject; they may however be used with native informants and second language learners (except when they are young children).

There are two other respects in which the student of interlanguage is in a favourable position. Unlike the investigator of child language he normally has a language in common with his subject, other than the language under investigation. Thus he can, for example, ask the subject to translate between his interlanguage and this shared language. This means the investigator normally has available an *authoritative interpretation* of the learner's utterances. Since the first necessity in making an analysis of any language data is that one should know what it means, this is clearly an advantage. Furthermore he can ask the subject to introspect about his interlanguage system. Neither of these methods is open to the investigator of child language, though, in favourable circumstances, they may be used by the linguist working with a native informant of an institutionalized language.

Thus while studies of the interlanguage of learners in formal settings are particularly hampered by the lack of spontaneously generated data, this is compensated for by the possibility of using a wide range of elicitation techniques.

I have been speaking so far as if the learning of second languages took place very largely in a formal educational setting. This is clearly not the case. Probably the overwhelming majority of bilinguals in the world have not learnt their second language in the classroom. In most multilingual communities throughout the world the learning of a second language takes place in an informal situation of language contact as a result of exposure to the second language being spoken by native speakers, conversing with each other or with the learner; that is, in situations resembling those in which the child acquires his mother tongue. In such settings the learner confronts the language as a means of conveying messages. He consequently pays attention to the most salient features of the speech signal in the first instance and bases his account of the language on these features. This is in striking contrast to the strategy of the learner in the classroom. Here the data is still largely written, does not betray clearly salient features, and is approached by the learner more as a structural, or formal, puzzle than as a semantic, or communicative, one. Furthermore in the informal setting the learner does not receive any treatment we would ordinarily call teaching. The language data to which he is exposed is not selected or organized in any way specifically to facilitate learning, although there is evidence that native speakers do modify their verbal behaviour in certain respects when conversing with foreigners. At all events the learner does not receive any help in the form of explanations, cues, or controlled practice. He may, however, receive some form of correction. This depends upon the social conventions of the community. But if he does, such correction is typically aimed at elucidating the learner's message rather than at correcting his formal errors. In such informal learning settings, one might expect that the interlanguage of learners would show different properties from that of learners in formal settings. And this is to a very large degree the case. But now we come to the crux of the problem: if there is indeed considerable variability in the properties of interlanguage found to occur in different situations of language learning, such as arise from differences in the age of the learner, differences in the mother tongue of the learner, and differences in the formality of the learning setting, what is the value of the concept of interlanguage? In other words, unless we can show some important formal properties which are common to the interlanguages of all second language learners in formal and informal settings and, equally, that the progressive development of their approximative systems towards some target language code follows a similar course, then the notion of interlanguage is a trivial one and we had better revert to the study of each second language learner, or second language learning situation, as something *sui generis*.

I believe that, short as is the history of interlanguage studies, the evidence is beginning to point to the conclusion that interlanguages as they develop, *particularly in the unstructured learning situation*, do bear resemblances to each other and that where variability exists, as it quite clearly does, it can be satisfactorily accounted for by appeal to particular features of the learning situation or the nature of the learner, as can the variability found in the language of infants acquiring their mother tongue.

It is necessary at this point to qualify this statement rather specifically. The resemblances which have been found are almost entirely syntactic ones. The phonology and phonetics of interlanguage have been extensively studied and invariably they show features related to the phonology of the mother tongue. At this level there is clearly interference. This can be accounted for by the transfer of the articulatory and perceptual habits of the mother tongue to the interlanguage, since the interlanguage phonological system created by the learner will be influenced by his phonetic habits. But the syntax he creates appears to be largely uninfluenced by his phonological system.

The claim I am making is, nevertheless, a powerful one, namely, that in the absence of attempts to control the learning process, as in the classroom, the sequence of development of the interlanguage syntax of learners, whatever their mother tongue and whatever the target language, will show general overall similarities particularly in the early stages. This claim implies that there is a property of the human mind which determines the way language learners process the data of language to which they are exposed, whatever the superficially different properties of the data may be. It is the object of interlanguage studies to discover what these processes are and what the 'natural' sequence of development is. This claim has motivated the call for longitudinal studies of language learners (particularly in informal learning settings) and already an impressive body of material has been accumulated. The argument is that if we can find some general principles of development, then these principles can be applied to the selection, organization, and sequencing of material for learning in a structured teaching situation. At the present time, whatever principles guide the organization and sequencing of instruction materials, they are not derived from any study of the psycholinguistic processes of second language acquisition. Hence the central relevance of interlanguage studies to applied linguistics.

The term interlanguage was introduced because learners' languages studied up to that time had regularly displayed formal features both of the target language and of some other language, notably, though not exclusively, of the mother tongue. The presence in learners' language of characteristics of the mother tongue has, as I pointed out, long been recognized, and has been accounted for by the psychological process of 'transfer'. More widespread studies of interlanguage development in recent years, to which I have just referred, have now shown cases where virtually no syntactic interference has been detected from the mother tongue, and where such interference as is found is not principally or uniquely from the mother tongue, but from some other second language known, however partially, to the learner. Furthermore it has now been well established that interlanguage may quite regularly exhibit systematic properties which show no obvious resemblance to the mother tongue or any other language known to the learner. In some cases interlanguage systems occur which are different from both the target and mother tongue even where these latter resemble each other. Sometimes we can account plausibly for these cases by showing that the learner is making false inferences about the target language as a result of the way that the target data has been selected or presented to him, or as a result of the way that he has been required to practise. In other cases no plausible explanations have suggested themselves.

Now, the study of learners' errors, and subsequently of interlanguage, as a phenomenon, was motivated, as I suggested, by a particular hypothesis about the processes of language learning. The results of these studies have tended so far to confirm the usefulness of this particular approach. The hypothesis is that the learner is creating for himself an account of the structural properties of the target language, about its grammar, on the basis of his interaction with the data he is exposed to. This account, which constitutes a sort of hypothesis about the data, is systematic and coherent and is, so to speak, his 'personal grammar' of the data. This hypothetical grammar of his requires confirmation or refutation. He tests its validity both receptively and productively: receptively, by using it for the interpretation of utterances made in the target language by his teachers or native speakers, and productively by using it to generate his own utterances, predicting that, if it is correct, his interpretation will be plausible in the context and his utterances will be accepted without comment or misunderstanding. If, on the other hand, his hypothesis is faulty, he will find his understanding is defective and his utterances will fail to communicate, and will be corrected. With whatever additional help he may get in the way of explanation or description, he elaborates, or restructures, his interlanguage grammar to accommodate the new information, and the cycle is repeated. Of course, in an informal learning setting he may not receive specific correction of his utterances; in such cases he may observe for himself that the forms he produces are not produced by native speakers; that is to say, his predictions, while not actively refuted, are nevertheless not positively confirmed. Furthermore he may profit by the correction applied to the utterances of fellow learners.

Now, clearly, I am not suggesting that learners are generally conscious of these processes, any more than we are consciously 'aware' of similar processes going on in our moment-to-moment interpretation of the sense data of perception with which we are continuously bombarded. After all, we only become aware of our misinterpretation of the nature of some feature of our environment when action on that interpretation leads to failure of some sort.

The learner continues, then, to upgrade, or elaborate, his understanding of the target language only so long as he has a motive for doing so. When his interlanguage grammar reaches that state of elaboration which enables him to communicate adequately for his purposes with native speakers, his motive to improve his knowledge or elaborate his approximative system disappears. Hence probably the phenomenon of 'fossilization', where a learner's interlanguage ceases to develop however long he remains exposed to authentic data in the target language. Most of us know foreigners in our community whose language has fossilized in this way in some respect or other. The process of fossilization may account for the stereotypic notions about the language of immigrant groups which we sometimes meet.

This outline sketch of the processes of language learning would suggest that the interlanguage grammars developed by all language learners should bear resemblances to each other, to the degree that there is similarity in the target data to which they are exposed. Furthermore, inasmuch as this account describes the process of acquisition of the mother tongue, as I believe it does, the sequence of interlanguage grammars exhibited by the infant and the second language learner should be similar. There is now strong evidence that in certain circumstances this is the case. Fairly large scale studies in the United States have shown that second language learning in young children, whatever their mother tongue, does show the same formal properties as the language development of infants acquiring that same language as a mother tongue. This has led some investigators to equate first and second language learning. However in the case of older children, either in a formal or informal learning setting, the influence of the mother tongue or other known languages becomes more evident, until, when we are dealing with adults, particularly if they are educated, interference seems to be strongest.

It appears then that the nature of the interlanguage grammar a learner creates for himself is to a considerable extent determined by the knowledge of language the learner already possesses and how elaborate or sophisticated that knowledge is. We can explain this informally by saying that the 'sense' we can make of any new experience is conditioned by the knowledge acquired from previous experience. In the case of second language learning, the more about language we know, or the more languages we know something of, the richer the repertoire of heuristic hypotheses available to us about the structural properties of the second language data will be. This would account for the similarities which interlanguages regularly show, not only to the mother tongue, but to other second languages known to the learner. Indeed it sometimes seems as if sophisticated adult learners unconsciously classify their experience of language into first and second languages and as a strategy prefer the hypothesis that a new second language is more likely to resemble a known second language than their native tongue.

There are other explanations for the variability in interlanguage grammars and indeed for the grammatical inconsistency found in the interlanguage of individual second language learners. In a formal learning situation it is usually assumed that the language data to which the learner is exposed is stylistically and dialectally homogeneous and internally consistent. The textual materials are normally written in the standard dialect of the target language and the correction offered by the teacher is based upon the standard language grammar. This is the ideal situation. But in many parts of the world this may not be the case. Not all teachers are native or near-native speakers of the target language. Many speak some form of interlanguage! Their own performance is therefore not always consistent in the target language or congruent with the textual material. Furthermore the learner may frequently be exposed to samples of target language data outside the classroom. This is particularly true of English as a second language. This may be some non-standard variety or quite frequently some form of English-related interlanguage; such would be the case of many immigrants to Britain.

Not only, therefore, are many learners exposed to inconsistent data but the range of possible heuristic hypotheses they may adopt about that data may be variable. This allows us to entertain the notion that a learner may adopt not just one hypothesis about the target language, but several concurrent hypotheses, leading to a set of coexistent approximative systems in his interlanguage. This again would show itself as apparent inconsistency in the grammar of his utterances. One must also allow for the possibility that the learner may utilize at least two interlanguage grammars, one for productive use and one for receptive use. There is some evidence that this is the case. But the methodological problem of investigating receptive interlanguage grammars is so formidable that we must maintain an open mind on the matter.

While variability in the characteristics of the interlanguage of language learners can be accounted for by appeal to the influences of inconsistent data, a variety of different heuristic hypotheses, and differing treatments in teaching, what requires explanation is the remaining marked similarities shown by the various approximative systems of learners *particularly in the earlier stages of learning and particularly in informal settings.*

I have already drawn attention to the dynamic, changing nature of interlanguages and noted that, save in those circumstances where they come to be used for communication between learners, as sometimes happens in schools for example, they are not institutionalized in a community. The principal striking characteristic of interlanguage systems is that they are, in linguistic terms, 'reduced' or 'simplified' systems, when compared with standard institutionalized languages. Furthermore they are restricted functionally in the uses to which they can be put. An older learner at least cannot effectively use his interlanguage for all the communicative purposes for which he uses his mother tongue. It is a matter for research at the present time to investigate the strategies that an interlanguage speaker adopts when faced with the necessity of communicating with his reduced approximative system. There is a connection between the formal properties of a grammar and what you can do with it, or between what you are trying to do and the grammar you choose to do it with.

The time has now come to draw together the various threads in my discussion on the phenomenon of interlanguage and to relate these to the practical task of language teaching. I have claimed that the concept of interlanguage is a useful one because in the process of learning a second language the approximative systems which learners create for themselves do, under certain circumstances, show interesting similarities. I have suggested that these similarities are evidence that certain basic processes are at work in the acquisition of a second language. Where there is variability, as there obviously is, then it must be accounted for by variability in one or another of the three elements in the learning situation: the learner, the setting, and the language involved.

The dimension of variability in the learner which is relevant is that of age. Young learners' communicative needs are more restricted than those of older learners, their experience of language is much less and perhaps their range of learning strategies is more restricted. Faced then with exposure to the second language they are more likely, whatever their mother tongue and whatever the target language, to develop a more similar set of approximative systems.

My first generalization then will be: other things being equal (that is, the formality of the learning setting and the identity of the target language) the younger the learners, the more similar the structural properties of their interlanguage systems will be.

The property of the learning setting that influences the nature of the interlanguage systems developed by the learner is that of formality. In a formal learning setting the focus of attention is still more on the acquisition of the target language code than on the use of the code in communication. The classroom does not encourage, or indeed easily permit, the free use of the interlanguage to create and receive messages. The learner therefore approaches the target language data in a fundamentally different way in a formal setting and in an informal setting. The free learner concentrates on the data's communicative properties – as a semantic challenge – while the captive learner approaches it as a structural problem – as a formal challenge.

My second generalization then reads as follows: other things being equal (that is the age of the learner and the identity of the target language) the more communicatively oriented the learning setting, the more similar the structural properties of the learners' interlanguage systems will be.

My last generalization is more speculative: if there are indeed universal properties in human language and if the process of language learning is one of complicating some sort of more simple, or basic, grammatical system, whatever the target language may be, then one would expect to find that in the earlier stages of learning any language, whatever the mother tongue of the learner, the approximative systems of the learners would show certain similarities. The evidence for this generalization is the striking similarities found in all simple codes, such as pidgin languages.

From these three generalizations one can predict, for example, that the maximum degree of similarity between approximative systems of learners will be found in the case of young learners of any language whatever their mother tongue in the earliest stages of learning a particular language in an informal setting, and *per contra* that the maximum differences in the approximative systems of learners will be found among adult learners of different mother tongues learning different target languages in formal settings. These two extreme predictions are borne out by the facts so far available.

Efficient language teaching must work with, rather than against, natural processes, facilitate and expedite rather than impede learning. Teachers and teaching materials must adapt to the learner rather than vice versa. The study of interlanguage is the study of the natural processes of language learning. What has been discovered so far suggests that the nearer we can approximate language teaching to the learning of second languages in an informal setting the more successful we shall be.

In practical terms this means two things. Firstly, the accommodation of the structure of our linguistic syllabuses and teaching materials to fit what is known of the sequence of progressive complication in the approximative systems of the free learner. Nickel (1973) has actually suggested explicitly teaching a sequence of approximative grammars of increasing complexity, in the way we in Britain use the initial teaching alphabet in the teaching of reading and writing. This of course means actually teaching what is regarded by native speakers as erroneous. This

suggestion, while interesting, is probably pedagogically unwork-
able at the present time since it is unlikely to be accepted by
teachers. What can be done is to adopt a more realistic attitude to
the language of the learner and by a selective correction of his so-
called errors attempt to teach only what his interlanguage system
permits him to learn at any particular moment.

More important, however, is a shift of emphasis in teaching away
from a preoccupation with the grammar of the target language
towards a concern with communication in the target language. The
progressive elaboration of the interlanguage system of the learner is
a response to his developing need to handle even more complex
communicative tasks. If we can control the level of these correctly,
the grammar will look after itself. Instead, then, of grading the
linguistic material that we expose the learner to, we should consider
grading the communicative demands we make on him, thereby
gently leading him to elaborate his approximative system. I believe
that educational theory and practice at the present time, with its
emphasis on learner-centred instruction, group learning, and
discovery methods, is ready to accept just such a shift of emphasis.
The actual techniques by which it is to be realized are the province
of the language teachers. This is the point at which the applied
linguist must hand over to his colleagues in the classroom and I
must draw my discourse to a close.

8 Simple codes and the source of the second language learner's initial heuristic hypothesis

Linguistic theory must be sufficiently rich and comprehensive to be able to account for the structure of the most complex or elaborate manifestation of language. In consequence any structurally less complex verbal behaviour is typically explained as a use of some 'reduced' or 'simplified' code or register. Many languages, if not all, are said to possess such reduced registers and it is said to be part of a native speaker's competence to be able to use such 'reduced registers' where appropriate. It is part of his total communicative competence to know when it is appropriate to use such registers. These reduced or simplified registers are associated with more or less well defined situations of language use or types of discourse. *Telegraphese* is obviously restricted by the medium of transmission as well as the restricted range of communicative functions it is used for, e.g. orders, reports, and announcements of plans. *Technical description* in botanical and ornithological reference books has a purely referential function, while the so-called *language of instructions* has clearly restricted rhetorical functions.

Baby talk (Ferguson 1964) has principally an affective function, as does, obviously, *lovers' talk. Foreigner talk* (Ferguson 1971, 1975) is said to be the code selected by native speakers when addressing foreigners who have little or no knowledge of their language. This is, however, rather doubtful and the evidence points rather to its principal use as one of ridicule. *Deaf talk* is situationally limited by the physical handicaps of the participants in the discourse.

All these codes are conventional and institutionalized in a language community, and systematic and more or less resistant to change as a result. They are said to be learnt by the usual processes of cultural transmission like any other part of the language. Any competent native speaker is able to produce appropriate discourse in these codes and interpret it when communicating, for the sort of specific purposes outlined above, with other members of the language community.

Another set of 'reduced languages' is represented by 'pidgins'. I use this term in the sense defined by Hall (1966), as a language system used by members of different speech communities, for certain restricted functions of communication for lack of a common code, but not the mother tongue of any speech community. In this case it is more difficult to assign a coherent sense to the terms 'reduced' or 'simplified', since the implication of such a description is that the speaker has available a more complex code of the same language, which he has, in some sense, simplified or reduced. This is manifestly not the case. Simplification or reduction is a term therefore which is implicitly comparative and used by an 'outsider' (the linguist) who sees the structure of a pidgin as related to some source language, by comparison with which it is structurally 'simpler' in some principled sense of the term.

A final type of reduced or simplified language is the interlanguage of the language learner, whether the infant learning his mother tongue or the second language learner. Neither of these interlanguages is normally institutionalized in a language community; *baby talk* and *foreigner talk* are stereotyped 'reduced registers' associated in the language community with these interlanguages. Interlanguages are in most cases too unstable to be institutionalized or to serve as social dialects. The speakers of these forms of language are not members of an 'interlanguage speech community' for whom the interlanguage is the 'norm' for communication, although 'outsiders' may seize upon certain structural properties for their own rhetorical purposes.

It is now indisputable that all three types of so-called simplified codes or languages exhibit strong structural similarities, the most salient of which are: a simple or virtually non-existent morphological system, a more or less fixed word order, a simple personal pronoun system, a small number of grammatical function words and grammatical categories, little or no use of the copula, absence of an article system (less often the absence of deictic words). The semantic functions of these and other systematic systems such as tense and aspect are typically performed, when at all, by lexical means, e.g. adverbs, or some 'imperial form'. The basic syntactic relations are expressed by word order.

Along with this basic syntactic system is found only a small lexicon with consequent heavy polysemy. That such systems can survive at all is accounted for by their use in severely restricted communicative functions, relying heavily for interpretation upon situational context. They can be seen in 'information theory' terms as being minimally redundant.

The significant features of these three types of 'simplified language' are summarized in the table:

Properties of three types of reduced languages

	Reduction	Admixture	Inter-group use
Pidginization	+	+	+
Reduced registers	+	−	+
Interlanguages	+	+	−

It is significant that in my attempt to characterize the properties of these 'reduced languages' or codes, I have been forced to use terminology which where not overtly comparative, e.g. *reduced, simplified, simpler*, is implicitly so, e.g. *a simple . . . no use of . . . absence of . . .* This implies that somehow what is 'natural' or 'basic' is a complex system and that these languages or codes are a reduction or a simplification of such a system. But it is precisely the aim of this paper to suggest that such an evaluative point of view is not only not relevant for the purposes I have in mind, namely explaining second language learning, but actually obscures an important fact. As I said at the beginning of this paper, linguistic theory must be so devised as to be able to account for any manifestation of language structure, the most complex as well as the least complex, however that complexity may be realized in any particular language system. For this reason linguists have always concentrated on describing the most complex forms of language (typically the standard written code) since all lesser or simpler systems could then be automatically accommodated. The types of code which I have enumerated above are examples of less complex language, but to characterize these as less complex does not entail that they have been simplified.

To use the terms 'simplified' or 'reduced' implies that a process of simplification or reduction has taken place. Now, simplification in this case may merely refer to the process carried out by the linguist in his description of these codes by comparison with the standard language, i.e. he uses the same set of categories and relations to describe both. These codes are rarely, if ever, described in their own terms but only in the terms needed to account for some more complex system. Simplification however may also refer to some psychological process in the speaker or learner of these codes. In other words there is some rule-governed psychological process for simplifying or reducing a complex internalized grammar. Samarin (1971) even hypothesizes that such rules may be universal:

'Would we find perchance that there was a universal intuitive notion of simplification?'

An alternative theory might be to turn the whole process upside down and treat 'standard' (i.e. complex) codes as 'complicated' forms of a 'basic' simple language, and then hypothesize that there are some rather general processes of 'complication', i.e. 'language learning'. I believe that this latter is a more fruitful and indeed plausible way of approaching the phenomenon of pidgins, interlanguages, and other 'reduced codes', though I should not of course wish to propose universal rules for 'complication'. On the contrary I would regard 'complication rules' as language specific. This proposal is obviously connected with the general belief that 'simple codes' are 'nearer', in some sense, to the underlying structure or 'inner form' of all languages, i.e. more overtly reflect semantic categories and relations (Kay and Sankoff 1972). Complex institutionalized languages represent therefore more or less distinct solutions to the problems of complication, while the motivation towards complication arises from the broadening range of communicative function within the speech community (Schumann 1975) and the need to reduce the ambiguity inherent in simple systems. Thus the development of a pidgin into a creole (the post-pidgin continuum) is one of progressive complication, as is also the development of an interlanguage through a series of more complex 'approximative systems' (Nemser 1971) into the target language, or the adult language in the case of the infant. Thus what I have classed as 'reduced registers' would represent fossilized intermediate approximative systems or stages in the complication process of a particular language which have become institutionalized and stereotyped. Such states need not all be at the same level of complication. This is evident from a cursory glance at the properties of the different 'reduced registers' of a single language. Thus foreigner talk, baby talk, and telegraphese are stereotyped in English, for example, at a less complex level than the language of instruction or botanical reference descriptions. This institutionalized fossilization of a code at different levels of complication can be regarded as a case of 'co-existent codes' (Tsuzaki 1971) or an interlingual continuum (Cave 1970). Descriptions of different degrees of pidginization within a single community are regularly available.

Jakobson (1968) draws our attention to the fact that even a child in full control of the complex adult code retains in his repertoire the code of an ontogenetically earlier interlanguage. He demonstrates this when he 'suddenly takes pleasure in reverting to the role of a baby and, either by imitating a younger brother or sister or to *some extent through his own recollection*, attempts once more to talk like one' (my emphasis). This interpretation is further supported by the frequent occurrences of a child 'regressing' to 'baby talk' in order to gain attention (Ferguson 1964). When this happens with adults we also speak of their using 'baby talk'. On this interpretation however the adult is not copying the infant's language but using a code which he himself internalized as an infant.

This suggests that the 'approximative systems' that all speakers of a language have passed through are not obliterated in the process of complication but remain available for use on what are socially approved occasions – hence the institutionalization of so-called 'reduced codes'.

A similar phenomenon can be regularly observed in the language classroom; both native and non-native teachers of a second language may frequently be heard to use an interlanguage which resembles to a greater or lesser degree the approximative system of their pupils. They are not in fact copying their pupils, but selecting a code they already possess from having internalized it at some point in their life. They do this of course only when real communication with their pupils is at a premium. In this case there is no institutionalization and, in the case of the native-speaking teacher, the code will certainly be influenced by the specific features of their pupils' interlanguage to which they have been exposed. In such a case we may speak of a contextually modified 'foreigner talk' (cf. cocoliche – an 'italianized' foreigner talk in Spanish). (Entwhistle 1936).

The hypothesis that I am proposing is that for any particular type of discourse in specific contexts a speaker adopts just that point on the simple-complex continuum which is complex enough for successful communication and that he 'shifts' up and down the scale as circumstances require. The process is however to some extent conditioned by social factors (e.g. the written code tending for obvious reasons towards the more complex end of the spectrum), the apparent exception, e.g. telegraphese, being simple rather than complex because of the restricted range of communicative functions it fulfils. This incidentally is one reason why foreigner talk is difficult to study – it is normally a spoken use of language occurring generally in short bursts and therefore it is difficult to collect sufficient data to make a systematic description. It may also be why the existence of these registers is not socially recognized and hence why they have received no generally accepted name (cf. cocoliche, for an exception), whereas pidgins are more generally accepted as existing as autonomous codes, and have names.

This may also be a reason why there is some difficulty on the part of language teachers to conceptualize the notion of interlanguages as autonomous systems. They tend to adopt the same attitude to them as was usually adopted to pidgins – i.e. deviant, distorted, or debased forms of some standard or target language.

The term interlanguage was originally introduced by Selinker to refer to a language system which he believed was intermediate between the learner's mother tongue and the target language on the grounds that it showed some formal characteristics of both. Interlanguages were unstable, i.e. always in the process of complication (except when they became 'fossilized') and consequently did not show the feature of institutionalization (though in some educational institutions, where the language of instruction is not the mother tongue, institutionalized school interlanguage pidgins regularly develop). It has since become clear however that the interlanguages of second language learners do not necessarily show evidence of 'transfer' from the mother tongue (Burt and Dulay 1974). The name interlanguage might therefore after all seem to be inappropriate to characterize the phenomenon, since it does not show in all cases obvious interlingual features. This has been found to be the case particularly among young children acquiring a second language without formal instruction, though there is little evidence that this happens with adults or older children, whether 'free' or 'institutionalized' learners.

I wish however to suggest that this inappropriateness is only apparent. I believe that this process of complication in language learning starts from a 'base', this base being literally a 'basic' language in which, for example, there is a simple relation between 'inner' and 'outer' form. Lyons (1973), referring to child language acquisition, says that 'much of the most recent research operates with the methodological assumption that the grammatical structure of the child's early utterance is determined primarily by such semantic notions as agency, animacy, and spatial location'. He goes on, 'It is plausible to hypothesize that the relatively simple grammatical rules that are required to analyse children's utterances are, if not universal, at least more general than many of the rules required for the analysis of adult speech, and that the more complex grammatical and semantic characteristics of adult language are developed on the basis of this earlier system'. He adds that this is a very traditional view.

The child evidently approaches the task of acquiring language by attempting to extract meanings from the utterances he is exposed to in context. It has often been pointed out that he probably first discovers a system in what is perceptually most salient, namely lexical items and sequence (Hymes 1971: 'The heart of pidginization is a focus on words and their order in situational context.'). From this he establishes his repertoire of basic syntactic relations and categories. It is on this basis that the process of complication starts in response to increasing communicative functional needs. Such a 'basic' language, Lyons suggests, may be universal. Now, I have already suggested that there is evidence that the process of complication does not 'obliterate' earlier systems and that these remain available to a speaker all his life for whatever purpose: communication or learning. Thus the child's 'basic' language can be regarded as the 'earliest' system we have. That we still have it is shown, for example, by our ability to interpret infants' utterances in context without too much difficulty.

When we come to learn a second language we thus have available this 'basic' system and, of course, an indefinite number of institutionalized more complex but still intermediate or approximative systems, notably the reduced registers of our mother tongue, together with, very often, fossilized approximative systems in other languages. Now it is often noted that in the learning of second languages the learner's interlanguage betrays evidence of interference not principally from his mother tongue but from other second languages he possesses, however imperfectly mastered (i.e. in some less complex approximative form). The evidence from error analysis is convincing here. My suggestion is, then, that in discovering the structure of the second language the learner uses as his 'initial hypothesis' (i.e. heuristic device) not necessarily the fully complex system of his mother tongue but rather one, or more, 'intermediate', less complex systems. This allows for the possibility of multiple hypotheses. (Inconsistency in 'errors' may be caused by this.) When faced with the data of the second language the learner adopts the same strategy as the infant, seeking meaning through analysis of what is most salient in the data, i.e. lexical items and sequence. On the basis of his 'initial hypothesis', i.e. whatever 'basic' heuristic system he possesses and selects, he interprets the structure of the data. This is the process of 'assimilation' in Piaget's sense and is essentially deductive. But what he attempts to assimilate the data to is not the complex structure of his mother tongue but some 'intermediate' form (i.e. a 'reduced' system). Since the 'intermediate' forms of all languages will bear stronger and stronger similarities to each other the nearer they approach the 'basic', possibly universal system, it is not surprising that the interlanguages of language learners, whatever their mother tongue background, will show formal similarities, and the nearer to the 'basic' form the 'initial hypotheses' are, the stronger the resemblance. Typically one may assume that children will start from a more 'basic' point and consequently the more similar the interlanguages will be whatever their mother tongues (Dulay and Burt 1974).

Evidence for the same process in the case of adults has been brought by Clyne (1968), who found amongst immigrant workers in Germany that their imperfect German (i.e. interlanguage) was a compromise between their own 'reduced registers' (whatever their mother tongue) and the 'reduced registers' (foreigner talk) of their hosts. Since they had different mother tongues their interlanguage served them as a 'lingua franca' and became institutionalized as a pidgin. (I am assuming here the Whinnom (1971) hypothesis for pidginization: tertiary hybridization – single target with multiple substrates.)

To summarize my argument. We have to account for the fact that all pidgins, 'reduced registers' in a single language, and the interlanguage of language learners all tend to show striking formal similarities, and secondly that in the case of the interlanguage of children learning a second language these show even more striking resemblances to each other, whatever their mother tongue, and to the intermediate grammars of the infant. All these phenomena can be explained if we abandon the notion of 'simplified systems' and substitute for it the notion of complication or 'complicated systems', and then hypothesize that no approximative system developed in the learning of any language is 'obliterated' but remains available both for special communicative functions in the mother tongue and as an 'initial' hypothesis in the learning of second languages.

9 Language continua and the interlanguage hypothesis

The term 'interlanguage', as we know, was introduced by Selinker in 1969 and elaborated in 1972 in an influential paper bearing that title, to refer to 'a separate linguistic system whose existence we are compelled to hypothesize, based upon the observed output which results from the (second language) learner's attempted production of a target language norm. This linguistic system we will call "interlanguage"'.

Although it is nowhere explicitly stated in his paper, it is evident that Selinker conceived of interlanguage as a 'dynamic system'. (For the notion of a continuum as a 'dynamic system' see Bickerton 1975). He makes it clear that he regards the 'interlanguage system' as the product of a psycholinguistic process of interaction between two linguistic systems, those of the mother tongue and the target language. He furthermore expounds at considerable length the notion of 'fossilization' which he characterizes as a 'mechanism' whereby 'speakers of a particular native language will keep certain linguistic items, rules, subsystems in their interlanguage, no matter what amount of instruction they receive in the target language'. Selinker therefore clearly conceived of interlanguage as being a *continuum*. He also explicitly recognized the process of 'regression', which he calls *backsliding*, when he speaks of 'the regular *reappearance* or *re-emergence* in interlanguage productive performance of linguistic structures which were thought to be eradicated'. He especially noted that such regressions are not random or necessarily towards the native language but towards an interlanguage norm. Note '*an* interlanguage norm' not '*the* interlanguage norm'. This makes it clear that the norm referred to is relative to an individual learner's language development, and not to some institutionalized code of a language community. Finally, he offers as 'part of a definition' of 'successful (second language) learning' that it is 'the *reorganization* of the linguistic material from an interlanguage to identify with a particular target language'. Other writers have referred to the same phenomenon and more explicitly recognized the language of the second language learner ·as a dynamic system; Nemser (1971) refers to a sequence of 'approxi-

mative systems' and allows that 'stable varieties of an approximative system are found' (for example among immigrant workers)
'where the learner has reached a plateau' in his learning. This is
similar to (but not identical with) Selinker's notion of fossilization.

It will be noted that the term *system* as used by Nemser
corresponds to the usual sense of the term as used by theoretical
linguists. The notion of a 'dynamic system' was not then available as
James (1974) made clear when he asked: 'How can a system remain
a system if it is in flux?'

What is, with hindsight, strikingly absent in Selinker's original
formulation is the notion of the interlanguage continuum as having
the property of increasing complexity or elaboration. There is
nothing in his original article which suggests that he saw the
interlanguage continuum as anything but a *restructuring* of the
learner's system from native language to target language *at the same
level of complexity*. A point of view clearly still held by Bickerton
(1975). It is only fair to add that other writers at the same period,
Richards (1971), the present author, and Nemser equally failed to
recognize movement along the continuum as possibly one of
progressive complexity. This was perhaps because we were all
concerned to describe and explain 'errors' of second language
learners and to investigate through them the processes or strategies
of second language learning, which we thought of as processes of
restructuring and accumulation, neither process alone necessarily
implying increase in complexity. The errors of learners were then
still largely believed to be due to transfer of features from the
mother tongue.

So long as the concept of an interlanguage continuum was one of
restructuring alone, it was bound to remain of relatively little value
or generality, since it could only be seen as movement between one
fully complex code and another. There were, therefore, as many
interlanguage continua as there were languages involved in the
learning situation and the sequences of restructuring would all be
different and the errors predicted by the theory would all be
'transfer' errors.

It is true that Richards (1971) refers to one hypothetical strategy
of language learners as *simplification*, thus implying perhaps that he
conceived of the interlanguage continuum as one of increasing
complication. However, he describes simplification as 'one way in
which speakers of different languages can make a new language
easier to learn and use' (Richards 1974). Since then many other
investigators of language learning have taken up the notion of
simplification as a 'strategy of learning'. This seems to me an
incorrect notion. Simplification may be the *result* of a learning

strategy or process: it cannot be a learning strategy itself, though it may well be a 'strategy of communication' (Widdowson 1977) i.e. how a speaker uses his knowledge in order to communicate effectively, equally no doubt true of native speakers as of interlanguage speakers and more obviously of *teachers* of second languages. It is important to my mind to keep quite separate, in the first instance, strategies of learning/acquisition and strategies of communication: the one referring to the mental processes whereby a learner creates for himself or discovers a language system underlying the data he is exposed to and the second the devices whereby he exploits whatever linguistic knowledge he possesses to achieve his communicative ends. All speakers, native or otherwise, adopt communicative strategies. Those of the interlanguage speaker have just begun to be investigated (Varadi 1973, Levenston 1971, Tarone *et al.* 1976).

There is, of course, an important connection between the two: (a) one of the motivations for developing an interlanguage must be that the speaker finds his strategies of communication inadequate for his communicative needs (James 1971, 'dialect expansion'), and (b) the data on the basis of which a learner creates for himself his interlanguage system is that produced by other speakers using *their* communicative strategies – these may be deliberately simplifying as perhaps a mother to a child, a native speaker to a foreign learner, or a teacher to a pupil, or in some cases another interlanguage speaker to the learner. This may account for some of the 'periphrastic' forms found in pidgins, since periphrasis is a typical communicative strategy. Note, however, that simplifying strategies of communication do not necessarily result in utterances which are formally deviant. A clear distinction must be made between a 'simple grammar' and utterances which are 'simple' to interpret.

Until evidence became available that learners of different mother tongues produced similar errors and thus that there were similarities in the many potentially different interlanguage continua, the interlanguage hypothesis lacked explanatory power. Such evidence has in the last few years come to light in ample quantities.

The evidence now points strongly towards the notion that the interlanguage of learners, whatever their mother tongues, in certain circumstances does go through a similar sequence of development at least in the earlier stages. This is now well established for children in informal learning settings, but evidence that it may also be true for adults in similar circumstances is also coming in (Perkins and Freeman 1975), and even for some adults in formal learning settings, and in spite of the learning syllabus imposed. Furthermore it is becoming clear that the interlanguage continuum is not simply one of progressive restructuring of the mother tongue systems and that the errors made by learners are not largely transfer errors, but that their utterances show evidence of a dynamic system similar to that of a child acquiring his mother tongue and may, at least to some extent, follow the same sequence of stages. Indeed it has been suggested that learning a second language is more of a recreative than a restructuring process (Dulay and Burt 1972) and thus similar to the acquisition of the mother tongue.

A revised definition of an interlanguage continuum might now read: a dynamic, goal-oriented language system of increasing complexity. Note that this definition does not specify that the continuum is institutionalized in any language community, i.e. language learners' (L_1 or L_2) interlanguage is not normally used for communication among themselves, although there do exist situations, e.g. second language medium schools, international summer courses, etc., when this may be the case. One might also include here immigrant workers in a country who share no common mother tongue, e.g. Gastarbeiter. In such cases some degree of stabilization or fossilization may be found (Clyne 1968). This is allowed for by both Selinker (1972) and Nemser (1971).

I shall call an interlanguage continuum a developmental continuum. I think it is fairly clear the defining properties listed above are also true of first language learners. It does not follow, of course, that the formal linguistic features of developmental continua should be the same, but it is an interesting fact that at least in the early stages they seem to be so, and this points strongly to a creative process as the common basis for both.

There are at least two other recognized continua which are candidates for this classification, the pre-pidgin and the post-pidgin (pre-creole) continuum. They are both goal-oriented in the sense that they both have a single target or reference language; they are both characterized by increasing complexity and can, like the interlanguage continuum, be described in terms of an implicational scale of features (De Camp 1971). However, they differ from L_1 and L_2 continua in that they are both liable to institutional-ization/stabilization. The speakers use the language for intercom-munication and, depending on the situation, the languages may become stabilized either because of the withdrawal of the model/target, or because they have reached the degree of complexity which serves the communicational or integrational needs of the speakers (cf. fossilization). The post-pidgin continuum comes into being by an expanded set of communicative or integrational needs (Schumann 1975) or by the reintroduction of a model/target (not necessarily the same one (cf. relexification)). I am inclined to regard these two continua as essentially one, since just as in the inter-language continuum, learning (development) may, for similar reasons, stop (absence of a model, satisfaction of communicational needs) or start again (availability of target language data, expanding communicational needs).

Once again it is an interesting fact that the formal linguistic properties of this continuum, especially at the earlier stages, should show similarities with those of the interlanguage continuum. The fact that there are similarities in the three developmental continua may be because they all involve learning, itself no doubt motivated by expanding communicative needs. But what is significant is the fact that the solution to the learning problem should in every case yield similar formal results in the early stages in what are otherwise disparate situations, i.e. the continua all seem to start from the same point. This strongly supports the view that all second language learning processes are more a case of recreation than restruc-turing.

I have classified the three continua so far considered as *developmental* because they all show the property of increasing complexity. But there are, of course, other language continua which do not show these properties. Studies of variability in language performance have now clearly shown that native speakers of fully complex codes vary their performance in principled ways in response to their perception of the social situation of interaction and in response to the different communicative tasks they are engaged on (e.g. degree of attention to form rather than content). It is now also becoming clear that a speaker of an L_1 or L_2 interlanguage also varies his performance within the range of options he has available. This may involve shifting to a code of equal complexity or a move down the scale of complexity. Children using their mother tongue have regularly been observed to 'regress' to earlier, i.e. less complex forms, when addressing younger siblings or 'playing up' to their parents. L_2 interlanguage speakers (including teachers!) have shown similar regression or 'backsliding' in their performance, and adaptation of their interlanguage to their communicative tasks (Dickerson 1975, Ervin-Tripp 1974). Similar variability has regularly been observed in pidgin speakers. Furthermore, adult native speakers who already possess a fully complex code may also in appropriate circumstances move down the developmental continuum to use such less complex systems ('simplified registers') as 'foreigner talk', 'baby talk' etc. (Ferguson 1971, Corder 1977a). It seems there is a dimension of variability in language use which we can call vertical variability to distinguish it from other forms of switching or shifting which have been more often described and which do not involve moving down the scale of complexity but rather across it. We might call the latter type horizontal variability.

It is this latter type of variability which has been so extensively studied by such scholars as Labov, Gumperz, Trudgill, and Bailey, and which permits us to speak of another type of continuum which we can call non-developmental or *lectal*. These continua are represented by dialect chains, sociolectal continua, or the decreolization (post-creole) continuum (Tsuzaki 1971, Bickerton 1975). They have in the past often been treated from a linguistic perspective as consisting of discrete linguistic systems, dialects, varieties, or registers of a language and have been correlated with movement through physical, social, or temporal space. From the point of the individual language speaker's repertoire, however, they represent an area within which his performance can range (individual polylectalism, individual bilingualism, etc.). These continua are to be distinguished from interlanguage continua in that they do not represent continua of progressive complexity. It is quite clear, for example, from Bickerton's studies that in the post-creole continuum he describes, his baso-, meso- and acrolect are of equal linguistic complexity and equal functional power. Thus the lectal continua can be described in terms of 'distance' (degree of restructuring) from some norm or standard recognized by the speaker, but not in terms of some degree of relative simplicity in relation to a target. The same is, of course, true of dialectal and sociolectal continua. Indeed the distinction in linguistic terms between all these lectal continua is unclear, if there is one at all. They do all share, however, the property of being reference-norm-oriented, in that the speakers explicitly or implicitly (by inference from their behavior) recognize as a norm some standard or prestigious form of the language, either by shifting in that direction in more formal interactional situations or deliberately shifting away from the norm when asserting social solidarity, or from evidence of hyper-correction. It is characteristic furthermore that productive command of a 'higher lect' usually gives the speaker some receptive command of a 'lower lect', but not always vice versa. In this respect they resemble interlanguage speakers who can 'regress' productively and receptively but cannot 'progress' productively though they may be able to do so receptively to some degree (Bickerton 1975).

The picture that emerges is one in which continua 'radiate' from a norm/target either in terms of restructuring at an equal degree of complexity or simplification to a decreasing degree of complexity.

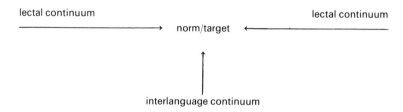

This model describes a space of at least two dimensions within which any speaker may move and within which his receptive and productive repertoire, or range, may be plotted (allowing, of course, for any discontinuities that may be found in his productive performance – e.g. split range, or diglossic, speakers). I have deliberately not described the norm as the standard dialect since the interlanguage target does not have to be a standard lect but may, of course, be any lect, as for example in the case of a learner whether as a first or second language of some non-standard form.

I shall now summarize. I have suggested that language is multi-dimensional, consisting of two basic types of continua – developmental, characterized by increasing complexity towards some particular target in the case of a language learner, and lectal (including dialect chains which also connect so-called different languages) characterized by equal complexity but oriented towards some reference-norm – in the case of any particular language community. I suggest that we can appropriately call the developmental continuum, the interlanguage continuum.

The original interlanguage hypothesis considered the interlanguage continuum as non-developmental, i.e. lectal, and by implication regarded second language learning as uniquely a restructuring process. My proposal now is that language learning, certainly in the case of a first language, is a creative process and yields in the individual a purely developmental continuum. In practice, second language learning in any particular individual is probably a mixture in varying proportions of restructuring and recreating. The evidence for restructuring is the occurrence in many cases and in certain situations of language acquisition of 'transfer errors', whereas the evidence for recreation is the absence of such errors and a preponderance of what may be called 'developmental errors' (e.g. over-generalization) similar to those found in first language learners' language.

It seems that our whole language teaching practice hitherto has been based upon the notion that second language learning follows a lectal or restructuring continuum. I suggest that it would probably be more realistic to accept that it is more 'natural' for it to follow a developmental or creative interlanguage continuum. Fundamentally, this is what Nickel (1973) suggested when he proposed teaching a developmental syllabus derived from a study of the progression of forms found in natural language learning situations, and also suggested by Widdowson (1977) when he proposed that the teacher's simplifications should be made to approximate to those of the learner at any particular stage in the learning process.

10 Language distance and the magnitude of the language learning task

A learner brings to the classroom many characteristics which are relevant to predictions about his career as language learner. These characteristics are the product of his membership of a community; he shares its language and its attitudes to, beliefs about, motivations for, and traditions in, language learning in general, and in the learning of specific second languages. And he possesses particular features of personality as formed by his personal history of maturation and experience. I am concerned in this chapter with the role of only two of these characteristics, both related to the community he belongs to: the nature of his mother tongue and any other languages known to him, and the beliefs current in his community, which he presumably shares, as to the nature, extent, and probable success in the learning task which lies ahead of him.

That members of a language community do hold certain beliefs about the magnitude of the task of learning specific second languages and their probable success in doing so is, I think, incontestable. That they can give some reasonable account of their assessment of the relative magnitude of the task of learning different foreign languages is highly probable. The British Foreign Service, for example, quantifies this task by paying different rates of language proficiency allowance, and also different subsidized periods of language instruction for its members, according to a scale of supposed or actually experienced difficulty in learning different groups of languages. This scale appears to correspond to what we may call a measure of 'linguistic' or 'structural' distance of any particular language from English. Thus languages classed as meriting entitlement to the highest allowance include Japanese, Burmese, Chinese, Korean, those to an intermediate allowance, Polish, Russian, Persian, and Turkish, while those attracting the lowest allowance include the usual European languages, such as Danish, German, and Spanish.

There are of course technical and theoretical problems in establishing and measuring degrees of language distance, but the assessment of the learning task undoubtedly correlates with some notion of genetic relatedness as established by studies of language typology. Thus it is reported and generally held that Persian is an easier language to acquire than Arabic, and German than Russian, for native speakers of English.

Kellerman (1977) has been investigating the notions that learners have about the 'transferability' of the forms of their mother tongue into second language performance. I would prefer to call this phenomenon 'borrowability', for reasons given later in this paper. It appears that learners may have quite clear (but, of course, sometimes mistaken) beliefs about what is similar in their mother tongue and the target language, and therefore 'borrowable'. In the earlier stages they seem to err in regarding the mother tongue as more unique than it is in fact. As he progresses the more realistic his assessment of the uniqueness of his mother tongue becomes and the more willing he is to borrow from it, or as we might say, the more realistic his assessment of language distance becomes.

I suggest, however, that the collective experience of a community of learning different foreign languages does lead to a reasonably realistic assessment of the relative magnitude of the learning task of acquiring any particular foreign language, and that this largely corresponds to the formal linguistic relatedness of the languages in question to the mother tongue.

This notion is, of course, not a new one and the explanation for it was held to be simple; the greater the degree of difference/distance, the larger the learning task, or to put it another way, the longer the learning path to be traversed between L_1 and L_2 (Lado 1961). This explanation, we may note, clearly assumed (a) that the starting point for learning was the mother tongue and (b) that the learning process was essentially one of restructuring. The more restructuring required, the longer the process, the greater the learning task. It is, of course, quite unnecessary to invoke any notions of comparative 'difficulty' in this explanation. The magnitude of a task is not logically connected with the measure of difficulty.

At this point we must narrow down the discussion to the acquisition of the syntax of the target language. There does seem to be good evidence that the acquisition of much of the phonology of the second language is essentially a restructuring process (Dickerson 1975). No one would seriously suggest that a second language learner replicates the phonological development of the infant acquiring its mother tongue. About the acquisition of vocabulary I have no proposals to make, except to suggest that this is very probably highly contextually dependent as it clearly is in the case of the acquisition of the mother tongue vocabulary.

The hypothesis, then, that learning the syntax of a second language is essentially a restructuring process was supported by the evidence that, particularly in the early stages of learning, as might be predicted, a greater degree of mother tongue features in the learner's interlanguage performance (hereinafter 'interference errors') are to be found. There are, however, two counter-arguments to this hypothesis. Firstly, by no means all learners show 'interference' errors in their speech and the amount of 'interference' varies considerably and unpredictably from learner to learner even under similar conditions of learning. Secondly, the restructuring hypothesis would predict that the learner's interlanguage grammar remained at an equal level of complexity at all stages of learning. This is so manifestly not the case that the restructuring hypothesis cannot be sustained.

The alternative hypothesis first proposed by the author in chapter 1 and since investigated by many other workers (Dulay and Burt 1973, 1974; Bailey, Madden, and Krashen, 1974; Larsen-Freeman 1975; Hatch and Wagner-Gough 1976; Hyltenstam 1977) was that learners had a 'built-in syllabus' for the learning of any particular second language. The natural cognitive processes of learning, when faced with a particular body of data, determined the sequence of creating that cognitive structure which we call the grammar of a language. The actual nature of the 'syllabus' or 'natural sequence', as it is sometimes called, was not at that time specified, since no empirical studies of second language acquisition had then been made, but there can now be seen to be two possible versions of the hypothesis of the 'built-in syllabus'. The *strong* version proposes that all learners of a given second language follow roughly the same development sequence whatever their mother tongue. The *weak* version proposes only that the development sequence is conditioned by the nature of the mother tongue.

There are two versions of the strong hypothesis: the $L_1 = L_2$ version (Dulay and Burt 1973), which claims that the development sequence is similar for the learning of a language both as a mother tongue and a second language, and another version, which merely proposes that there is a particular 'natural sequence' common to all second language learners without specifying whether this is similar to the sequence of the mother tongue learner.

The arguments against the strong version are that, if it is true in either of its forms, then (a) any given L_2 should present an equal learning task, since it is assumed that whatever the route, the end points, fully complex natural languages, are equally complex. There is no evidence that natural languages vary in their overall complexity. Normal infants acquiring their mother tongues all take much the same time to reach the same levels of communicative competence. Since it is manifestly not the case that all languages do present the same learning task to speakers of all mother tongues the strong version of the 'built-in syllabus' hypothesis appears to fail. (b) If the mother tongue plays no part in the acquisition of the second language then one must find some alternative explanation for 'interference' phenomena in the learner's speech. This, I believe, it is possible at least partially to do. See below. It does not, however, follow logically that if 'interference' phenomena are absent, the mother tongue (and other languages) plays no role in the learning process. See also below.

The arguments against the weak version of the 'built-in syllabus' hypothesis are, however, equally cogent. (a) We have to explain away the now very considerable evidence that learners, child and adult, free learning and under formal instruction, do appear to go through sets of largely similar developmental sequences whatever their mother tongue (for a discussion of relevant research see Krashen 1977). If the 'built-in syllabuses' were indeed conditioned by the nature of the mother tongue then developmental sequences would be predicted to differ considerably in the cases of learners having various, structurally different, mother tongues. This has not yet been shown to be the case. (b) The weak version of the hypothesis would also predict that 'interference phenomena' would be similar and constant for all learners of particular mother tongues under all conditions of learning. This has also not been found to be the case (Clyne 1968, Dulay and Burt 1973).

It appears then that neither the strong nor the weak form of the 'built-in syllabus' hypothesis (i.e. re-creation hypothesis) can be sustained in its simple form. What is needed for an adequate model of second language acquisition is a hypothesis which can reconcile the following relevant findings:

1   The variability of the occurrence of 'interference phenomena' in differing learning conditions.

2   The considerable similarity of the sequential development of learners of different mother tongues when acquiring certain aspects of some particular second language.

3   The relative different magnitudes of the task of learning different second languages in relation to different mother tongues of learners.

I shall take each of these points in turn.

1   The notion of 'negative transfer' has generally been invoked to account for the occurrence of 'interference phenomena' in interlanguage speech. It was also allowed that the mother tongue

might have a 'facilitating' effect where L_1 and L_2 systems resembled each other ('positive transfer'). It was generally assumed that 'interference' or 'inhibition' and 'facilitation' were two sides of the same coin. In fact of course this is not a logical necessity. The characteristics of the L_1 may 'facilitate' or 'not facilitate' but 'failure to facilitate' is not equivalent to 'interfere' or 'inhibit'. It is perfectly logical to propose that the nature of the L_1 may make passage along the built-in syllabus faster when it bears similarity to L_2, but simply has no effect when it is different. In such a case the learner is left with his own unaided cognitive learning capacities to discover those aspects of the L_2 which are not similar to his L_1. Facilitation clearly does not lead to 'interference phenomena' in the learner's speech, but neither does non-facilitation. The errors made in either case will be developmental not interference errors; in the case of facilitation, however, one may expect that the quantity of developmental error will be less since passage through the syllabus will be accelerated. Where then do 'interference errors' come from?

An entirely plausible and commonsensical answer has long been available. A learner when faced with the need to communicate will have recourse to whatever linguistic knowledge he has which will increase the likelihood of successful communication. (Corder 1973). If he lacks the requisite knowledge of L_2 to achieve successful communication then he will have recourse to the L_1 or any other language he knows to make up this deficiency – beg, borrow, or steal. And the greater the deficiency, typically at the beginning of a course, the greater the amount of borrowing (Taylor 1975). As Newmark said: interference is simply the result of a performer being 'called upon to perform before he has learnt the new behaviour. The result is "padding", using old knowledge, supplying what is known to make up for what is not known.' (Newmark 1966, quoted by Krashen). And he adds 'the cure for interference is simply the cure for ignorance: learning'. This is another way of saying that the motivation for the complexification of the interlanguage is the pressure of communicative needs (Valdman 1978).

It is now customary to make a distinction between 'learning strategies' and 'communicative strategies'. 'Transfer' has usually been invoked as a learning strategy – the incorporation into the interlanguage grammar of mother tongue systems. We must remember here the original meaning of 'transfer' in psychology – the persistence of, or resort to, already existing behaviour in a functionally new behavioural activity. Let us also remember that 'transfer' was a concept in behavioural learning theory and referred specifically to what would now be called features of 'performance'.

Competence or underlying cognitive structures have no place in such a theory.

The notion, however, of 'transfer' as a learning strategy would account for the generation of sentences having mother tongue-like features, which, if the L_1 system were not identical with the L_2, would be counted as 'interference errors'. If similar, of course, transfer features would pass unnoticed. The alternative hypothesis outlined above treats 'interference errors' as more or less ad hoc *unsuccessful* borrowings to 'pad out' the gaps and inadequacies of the interlanguage system when faced with communication problems – that is, the result of a communicative strategy. This account, of course, has two advantages: (a) it explains the varying degree of 'interference' found among learners with otherwise similar learning conditions and knowledge, i.e. it relates 'borrowing' firmly to communicative needs and actual performance and (b) it accounts for the relative consistency of the *types* of unsuccessful borrowing (interference errors) and relates the known or predictable gaps in the 'built-in syllabus' at various stages to the available 'paddings' from the L_1 or other known languages. The more demanding the communicative activity required of a learner (i.e. the greater the mismatch between 'means' and 'ends', 'knowledge' and 'need') the greater the amount of borrowing in general and hence of unsuccessful borrowing (interference error).

We may note here that 'interference errors' are strongly associated with classroom language activity (I will not dignify it with the title of communication) and this is what would be predicted where it is not the learner himself who controls the nature of this activity. In a free communication situation a learner can adopt all sorts of alternative strategies to 'borrowing' which are generally deprecated or banned in the classroom, e.g. gesture, guessing, periphrasis, semantic avoidance, etc. (Tarone *et al.* 1976).

2   The second finding we have to account for in the theory is the strong similarity observed in the sequential development of some aspects of learners' interlanguage from differing mother tongues (Hyltenstam 1977). I have already suggested in previous chapters that the starting point of the language learning continuum is a basic, simple, possibly universal grammar to which all language users have access, because in the process of language acquisition every infant creates such a simple grammar. We have access to this grammar because we do not forget our own linguistic development; we do not kick away the ladder by which we climb, but are able under certain circumstances to utilize such grammars for communicative purposes as adults (e.g. foreigner talk, baby talk, etc.) and

also for second language acquisition (Traugott 1973, Ervin-Tripp 1974). It cannot be an accident that the early stages of both L_1 acquisition, L_2 acquisition, 'simplified registers', and pidgins all show striking formal similarities. This hypothesis has already received considerable support from the studies of morpheme acquisition (Schumann 1975) in adults and children in second language acquisition.

3   Thirdly, what we must also account for is the relative different speeds of learning different second languages in relation to various mother tongues. As has been suggested, the time taken or the learning task faced by an infant acquiring any language is assumed to be of approximately equal magnitude. All infants achieve similar levels of communicative competence at approximately the same stage of development. If then second language learners are engaged upon the task of creating for themselves a grammar of any particular second language, all starting from the same point, and apparently all following the same development sequence thereafter, why is it that they typically take different times over the job? Why is it that apparently the same task differs in magnitude for different groups of learners? The hypothesis here proposed states that, other things being equal (e.g. motivation and access to data, etc.), the mother tongue acts differentially as a facilitating agency. Where the mother tongue is formally similar to the target language the learner will pass more rapidly along the developmental continuum (or some parts of it), than where it differs. Genetically related languages are assumed to share a large number of rules, particularly in the deep grammar, differing principally in the more superficial aspects. Passage along the developmental continuum is therefore rapid until those relatively superficial distinctions are met, whereas in the case of unrelated (distant) languages differences exist along the whole developmental continuum, slowing down the speed of acquisition. This hypothesis is testable by a comparative study of learners acquiring two different languages simultaneously under the same learning conditions, e.g., exposure, teaching, motivation, etc.

We must remember here that not only the mother tongue may be facilitative. Other languages known to the learner, however imperfectly, may, in the degree to which they resemble the target language structurally, have a facilitating effect. This hypothesis is supported by the very general observation that the more languages one knows the easier the acquisition of yet another appears to be. This is usually explained by the notion that in such cases the learner has a larger number of 'ready-made' hypotheses to test in processing the data of the new language. Let us note here in parentheses that the possession of a number of languages may actually act as a facilitating agency in the manner just suggested but also provide an increased resource for 'borrowing' as a communicative strategy.

In summary, the model of the learning process that emerges is one in which the learner starts his learning programme from a basic, possibly universal grammar which he proceeds to elaborate in response to his exposure to the data of the target language and his communicative needs. The elaboration follows a more or less constant sequence for all learners of a particular language but any particular learner's progress along the developmental continuum is significantly affected by the degree to which his existing knowledge of language may facilitate his advance. This facilitation does not manifest itself in the transfer of mother tongue features to his interlanguage grammar, but in the more rapid discovery of the mother tongue-like features of the target language. Where unacceptable mother tongue-like features appear in his speech they are the result of an unsuccessful communicative strategy of 'borrowing'. All of us, in other words, already know the second language to a greater or lesser extent. Part of the task of acquiring a second language is finding out how much we already know of it. The more we find we know, the less the magnitude of the learning task.

11 Strategies of communication

Strategies of communication were first invoked by Selinker (1972) in his paper entitled 'Interlanguage' to account for certain classes of errors made by learners of a second language. These errors were regarded as a by-product of the attempt of the learner to express his meaning in spontaneous speech with an inadequate grasp of the target language system. Varadi (1973) was the first to investigate this phenomenon experimentally but little work has since been published on the topic; the most recent attempt to provide a framework for analysis of strategies of communication is Tarone, Cohen, and Dumas (1976). It is now fairly clear that all language users adopt strategies to convey their meaning, but we are only able more or less readily to perceive these when the speaker is not a native speaker.

The strategies adopted by speakers, of course, depend upon their interlocutors. What we attempt to communicate and how we set about it are determined not only by our knowledge of the language but also our current assessment of our interlocutor's linguistic competence and his knowledge of the topic of discourse. But both these are variable and actually may change and develop in the course of ongoing interaction. Furthermore since communication is a cooperative enterprise, one must suppose that we may adopt both productive and receptive strategies of communication. So far no one has attempted within the framework of interlanguage studies to investigate the latter.

Studies of communicative strategies have therefore largely concentrated on productive strategies of language learners interacting with native speakers of the target language, where the simplifying assumption has been made that the interlocutor has 'perfect' command of the language system and also 'perfect' command of the topic of discourse.

A working definition of communicative strategies is that they are a systematic technique employed by a speaker to express his meaning when faced with some difficulty. Difficulty in this definition is taken to refer uniquely to the speaker's inadequate command of the language used in the interaction. This again is obviously a simplifying assumption, but one which permits a start to be made on investigating a difficult topic.

Much of the literature in the field seems to me to lack a general view of the problem and one of the principal confusions found is between what are called strategies of learning and strategies of communication. Some authors appear even to regard these expressions as nearly synonymous. Perhaps one of the reasons is that in both cases the data for investigating are the same, namely utterances in the interlanguage of the speaker. It is frequently difficult therefore to identify a particular feature of an utterance unequivocally as the result of one or the other strategy, i.e. the result of the learner's interlanguage system or an ad hoc result of some communicative strategy. This is particularly the case with features of an utterance which bear a resemblance to features of the speaker's mother tongue. They may be regular characteristics of his language at the time of study, in which case they could be supposed to result from the interlanguage grammar which he has created for himself, and are therefore the product of a strategy of learning which utilizes the mother tongue system as a heuristic technique. This is the feature often called 'interference' and the strategy of learning which produces it is the strategy of 'transfer'. On the other hand an interlanguage speaker may, in his attempts to communicate, simply 'borrow' for immediate purposes items or features of his mother tongue (or any other language he knows) without incorporating them into his interlanguage system. 'Successful borrowing', that is when a 'borrowed' item is 'accepted' by the interlocutor as 'well formed' in the target language, may lead to that item being incorporated into the speaker's interlanguage repertoire. This could be regarded as 'learning'. As Hatch (1978) says: 'Language learning evolves out of learning how to carry on conversations'. 'Unsuccessful' borrowings of course will be rejected. It is because of this interaction between strategies of communication and strategies of learning that the confusion I spoke of may have arisen.

Strategies of communication are essentially to do with the relationship between ends and means. In a native speaker it is assumed that these are ideally in balance, that is that he always has the linguistic means to express the messages he wishes to communicate. In a learner, however, these are not in balance. The learner will sometimes wish to convey messages which his linguistic resources do not permit him to express successfully. When in the course of interaction the learner finds himself faced with this situation, he has only two options open to him. He can either tailor his message to the resources he has available, that is adjust his ends to his means. These procedures we can call *message adjustment strategies,* or risk-avoidance strategies. Or he can attempt to increase his resources by one means or another in order to realize his communicative intentions. These strategies we can call *resource expansion strategies.* These are clearly 'success oriented' though risk-running strategies. If one wishes at this stage of the art to consider the pedagogical implications of studying communicative strategies, then clearly it is part of good language teaching to encourage 'resource expansion strategies' and, as we have seen, successful strategies of communication may eventually lead to language learning.

Students of communicative strategies have identified (in a provisional way) a number of communicative strategies and they will all be found to fall into one or the other of these two macro-strategies. Thus among *message adjustment strategies* we have at one extreme 'topic avoidance', a refusal to enter into or continue a discourse within some field or topic because of a feeling of total linguistic inadequacy. A less extreme form of topic avoidance would be 'message abandonment': trying but giving up. A less acute form of message adjustment is 'semantic avoidance', that is saying something slightly different from what you intended but still broadly relevant to the topic of discourse. Finally the least acute form of message adjustment would be 'message reduction', that is saying less, or less precisely what you intended to say. This is often seen as rather vague general talk.

These strategies must not be regarded as admission of failure. Let us remember that in face to face interaction it is frequently essential from a social point of view to maintain interaction with your interlocutor. To say something is often just as important as to say what you would actually like to say!

When we turn to the *resource expansion strategies* the situation is different. Here we cannot order the techniques according to a hierarchy. We frequently find one or more strategies being employed simultaneously. All are risk-taking, in that they run the danger of failure, i.e. misunderstanding or communication breakdown. The most obvious strategy, that of 'borrowing', has been mentioned, i.e. the use of linguistic resources other than the target language, but this includes guessing of a more or less informed kind, that is, an attempt to use invented or borrowed items, all more or less approximated to the rules of the target language structure as far as the learner's interlanguage allows. The extreme form of borrowing is of course simply 'switching' to another language – the most risky enterprise. While a less risk-taking strategy is to use paraphrase or circumlocution, that is getting round your problem with the knowledge you have, which is inelegant perhaps, but successful. One must not forget here a resort to paralinguistic devices as a resource-expansion strategy (typically, gesture) or to appeals for help from the interlocutor for a word or expression, which is the least risk-taking strategy of all.

How are these strategies manipulated? There is some evidence that there is a personality factor involved. Different learners will typically resort to favourite strategies – some are determined risk-takers, others value social factors of interaction above the communication of ideas, but one may assume that there is a general preference for maintaining one's intended message. Just how hard one tries will vary with personality and speech situation. One can then propose the following *encoding routine* at least as a testable hypothesis.

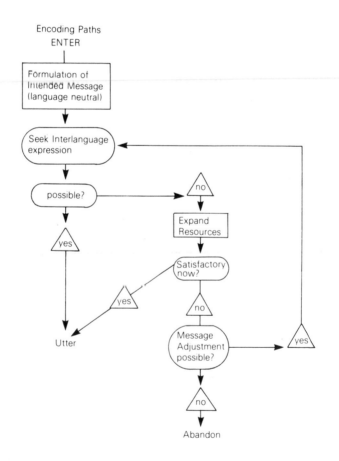

12 Formal simplicity and functional simplification

It is part of the competence of all adult speakers of a language that they can accommodate their way of using the language, that is their rhetoric (and where conventionally appropriate their grammatical code), to their interlocutors in a socially sanctioned manner. Such an accommodated rhetoric is what is generally referred to by the term *register*. This accommodation also takes place where the interlocutors are infants or foreigners; the common feature of these two being that they have not yet mastered their respective target language systems, the adult code in the case of the infant, the second language code in the case of the foreigner. From the now considerable research into mothers' speech to children (Snow and Ferguson 1977) (mother talk, motherese, caretaker talk, etc.) and to a lesser extent native speakers' (including language teachers') speech to foreigners (let us call it teacher talk) (Henzl 1974, 1975, Gaies 1978, Hatch *et al.* 1976b) it is now emerging that these accommodations of rhetoric, which result in what are identified as two registers, are quite similar in a number of respects and both, in their turn, are the result of an overriding necessity in their speakers to communicate successfully with interlocutors who are defective in their knowledge of the language system. The characteristics of these registers are as they are in order to make the task of receptive processing maximally efficient, to make it as *simple* a task as possible. Neither appears to have as its primary function that of facilitating the acquisition of the language. This is well established, at least in the case of mother talk; work on teacher talk has not yet proceeded far enough to be certain. There appears, in other words, to be no statistical relation between the input and the output in child speech (Brown 1977). I would, in parenthesis, expect a similar finding in the case of native speakers' speech and language learners' speech, at least outside the classroom (cf. Traugott 1977). A high frequency of particular syntactic structure is not expected to be reflected in the acquisition of that structure by the foreigner.

These two registers, mother talk and teacher talk, are often characterized as being in some way simplified. The term 'simplified' in this case implies both a comparison and a process and can be glossed as 'has become or been rendered simpler than . . .' That is to say, mother talk or teacher talk are simpler than other registers of talk, such as, for instance, that used between native speaking adults. In this sense, mother talk and teacher talk can be regarded as 'marked' registers since the talkers are capable of, and 'normally' use, a more complex register and thus can properly be regarded as *simplifying* their rhetoric when interacting with infants or foreigners. *Simplified* in this context can only mean 'simple to process by receiver', cf. Slobin's 'ground-rules' for intelligibility (Slobin 1973). It has no implications as to the complexity of the language system or code, as I shall hereafter refer to it.

On the contrary, study of these registers has shown that normally the grammar underlying them is the fully complex adult grammatical code; i.e. there is no evidence of 'broken', ungrammatical, pidgin, or interlanguage-like forms. (For a discussion of the grammaticality of mothers' speech see Newport *et al.* (1977) who say it is 'unswervingly well-formed'.) There is no evidence, in other words, that the code used is structurally simple[1]. What there is evidence for (Henzl 1974), however, is that simplified registers involve a selection by the speaker out of the total repertoire of forms generated by the grammar of their complex code. This means that certain forms and structures may be less frequent or completely absent in a simple register. This, however, does not mean that the *code* is being simplified, only that the *use* is being simplified. It is this fact which has led to the frequent confusion between codes and registers and has led people to use such terms as foreigner talk indifferently to refer to a code and a register. One may add that this selective process is true of any register of a language, but does not in other cases lead to their being characterized as simplified, because such a process does not have the effect of their being more readily processed by the interlocutor, e.g. 'lawyers' talk'.

It will be immediately apparent that I am here insisting on a fundamental distinction, which is regularly blurred in discussion of *simplification*, between usage and use (Widdowson 1978) or between the *use of a structurally simpler grammar or code* such as foreigner talk code or baby talk code (which is regarded as 'ungrammatical' by comparison with the fully 'normal' complex code) and the *simplified use of a fully complex code* such as mother talk or teacher talk. It is a historical misfortune that the term *talk* has been, and regularly still is, used to refer indifferently both to language systems (or codes) and to the uses of language systems (or registers); this has led to much confusion as a result. *Talk*, I suggest, should preferably be reserved for a rhetoric, that is a use of language (register).

It is nevertheless the case that these *simple codes*, just as the *simple registers*, are typically associated with certain specialized language functions by native speakers. Thus foreigner talk code is typically used to characterize or mock foreigners' speech and baby talk code to speak to pets, mental defectives, and lovers. In this sense the adoption of a simple code may also signal a shift of register. It may also be the case that these codes are occasionally selected to speak to foreigners or infants respectively. When this happens it is probable they carry some marked affective or social meaning (Brown 1977, Meisel 1977, Ferguson and de Bose 1977). That is, they mark a special relationship between the interlocutors, e.g. loving mother to child, native boss to foreign worker.

It is part of the competence of native speakers to know when a *register shift* also involves a shift down the continuum of grammatical complexity (see chapter 9), that is, a concomitant *code shift*.

I have so far identified two distinct meanings for *simple* or *simplified*; the first, a psycholinguistic meaning signifying 'simple for receiver to process' used in connection with registers, and the second, a comparative descriptive linguistic meaning signifying 'structurally simple', used to refer to codes. I have also suggested that there is no logical connection between these two. I now want to make a further important distinction: that between state and process. Thus, the term *simple* is properly used to refer to some state or characteristic of something, e.g. a code or a register is simple by comparison with some other code or register. *Simplified*, on the other hand, refers properly to the result of a process of simplification, one of shifting, selecting, or modifying a code or register to render it perceptually or structurally simpler.

Thus one can, as I have suggested, refer appropriately to mother talk as a *simplified register* inasmuch as the speaker has modified or accommodated her usual complex inter-adult rhetoric in order to make her speech simpler for her infant interlocutor to process. Similarly, one can also properly speak of a native speaker's code shift towards a structurally simpler code as a simplifying step or process, since he is shifting from his normal complex code to something structurally simpler. In the mouths of native speakers, therefore, a shift to foreigner talk code is indeed a simplifying step or process, and foreigner talk code is therefore appropriately designated a 'simplified code'. It has indeed been suggested that it is part of every native speaker's competence to be able to simplify his code in this way (Traugott 1973, Ferguson 1971, Bickerton 1977) and there may be general, perhaps universal rules for doing so (Samarin 1971). The structural similarity between all simple codes in all languages and pidgins does indeed support such a hypothesis.

The contrast between these two notions of state and process is found in the term *pidgin language*, on the one hand, referring to a particular type of supposedly simple language code, and the process of *pidginization*, on the other, which refers to a linguistic process whereby some superstrate language undergoes a process of simplification, i.e. when superstrate language L is pidginized, the process results in a *simpler* code, Pidgin P, related to and derived from it. The universe of discourse in which the term 'pidginization' is used is comparative structural linguistics. Pidginization is a linguistic, *not* a psycholinguistic, process and cannot properly be used to refer to the process whereby pidgins are created by speakers of other languages acquiring them on the basis of exposure to the data of the superstrate language. This is a different problem altogether and is regarded by Bickerton (1977) as 'an exercise in second language learning under extremely adverse conditions'. This cannot, I suggest, be properly referred to as a process of simplification for the reason that it does not represent a 'code shift' by the speaker. An incipient pidgin speaker clearly does not, *by definition*, command the superstrate code (if he did he would not be a learner but a native speaker). He cannot therefore be said to be 'simplifying' in a psycholinguistic sense.

It is my argument, therefore, that if in the process of first or second language acquisition the learner demonstrates that he is using a simple grammar or code, as is well attested, then he has not arrived at that code or grammar by a process of simplification of the target code. In other words, you cannot simplify what you do not possess. To refer, therefore, to the learner's interlanguage as *simplified*, or to speak of the process of first or second language acquisition as in part, or in the earlier stages, one of simplification is highly misleading and to do so is to show a serious confusion between what Valdman (1977a) calls an 'evaluative linguistically oriented view' on the one hand, and an attempt to account for the psychological processes and strategies of language acquisition on the other. A similar point is made by Traugott (1977) who calls the use of the term simplification in this case a 'metatheoretical concept resulting from a static comparative view of language'. This is, then, I suggest, an unfortunate confusion regularly indulged in and hinders a proper investigation of the difficult problem of what language learners' strategies and processes may be.

It is my suggestion and one which accords with all that we know of language acquisition that it is essentially one of *elaboration* or *complexification*, not one of simplification. But this suggestion, of course, merely shifts the problem to that of determining what it is that the learner is elaborating, that is, to what the learner's starting point may be, and to this I now turn.

Second language learners have by definition already learnt a language and in most cases already possess the fully complex code of their mother tongue (if they do not they are probably acquiring a second first language). We are, therefore, absolved from getting involved in any controversy which may still persist about the starting point of first language acquisition (nativist versus interactionist hypotheses). Everything we know about human learning makes it highly implausible to suppose that a second language learner will simply replicate in detail the whole language learning process he has already gone through in acquiring language, and that no recourse whatsoever is had by him to existing knowledge, especially his knowledge of the adult functions of language. The problem of the starting point is therefore precisely to determine *what* use the second language learner does make of his knowledge and experience of language in use when confronted with the task of acquiring and communicating immediately in a second language.

We can, of course, immediately rule out any hypothesis which proposes that, at the syntactic level at least, his starting point is his fully complex mother tongue system and that he is engaged in progressively modifying or 'restructuring' this system in the direction of the target system (Nemser 1971, Selinker 1972). If this were the case his interlanguage system in the early stages would be highly complex, since his mother tongue is highly complex. This is manifestly not the case. It is, all are agreed, extremely simple. A restructuring process is not one of elaboration.

There remain then two possibilities: that he starts from scratch like an infant acquiring his mother tongue or that he starts from some simple basic grammar. All the evidence and what we have said above argues against the first solution. We are therefore left, however improbably, with the notion that there is some basic, simple, possibly universal, code as the starting point for second language acquisition, a language-neutral 'natural semantax' as Traugott (1977) has called it. If we entertain this notion we are under an obligation to propose how the learner knows or acquires such a natural semantax. There are two possible answers to this problem: either he has learnt such a code from his contact with simple codes in regular use in his community, e.g. foreigner talk, baby talk, or various other simple codes (Ferguson 1971) or he knows such a code by virtue of having himself been a language learner once already; i.e. he has inevitably created such a code for himself in the process of language acquisition and retained that knowledge. This suggests that language learners regress to an earlier stage in their own linguistic development before starting the process of elaboration, that they have access to the knowledge created in their own linguistic development.

Putting it this way could be regarded as an alternative way of expressing Samarin's suggestion that we all 'know' the 'universal rules' for simplifying grammars. Such an idea is, of course, not new, and has been regularly expressed by those working on the development of pidgins, (cf. Traugott 1973, Bickerton 1977, Ferguson and De Bose 1977, Ervin-Tripp 1974, etc.). Some typical expressions of this view are:

> 'Part of the communicative competence is the ability of incipient speakers of a language to make themselves understood in a language of which they know mainly a reduced set of basic vocabulary items.' (Ferguson and De Bose 1977, p. 117)

> 'Does it not involve the acquisition of lexical items so typical of adult innovation, combined with a return to earlier processes, especially syntactic ones that have in the speaker's language been partially or wholly repressed?' (Traugott 1973, p. 318)

> '(Children learning a second language) . . . 'regress' to a processing strategy still available to them for use under certain conditions . . . (in their mother tongue).' (Ervin-Tripp 1974, p. 126)

> 'A plausible inference from the facts is that these are universal principles of linguistic simplification that appear under specifiable conditions. Among these conditions may be the use of language in restricted social settings and by non-native speakers (both conditions apply to pidgins) and the use of language by the immature novice.' (Newport et al. 1977, p. 135)

Further support for this argument is found in the facility which quite young children demonstrate to revert to earlier and simpler codes (baby talk) when interacting with infant siblings (cf. Traugott 1977, Jacobson 1968, Schatz and Gelman 1977). This suggests that these basic simple codes are indeed not *learnt* but *remembered*, and access to them may be triggered by rather special interactional situations such as second language learning and the need to communicate at all costs (cf. pidgins).

To conclude: if simplification plays any part in second language acquisition as a process or learning strategy then *it is not the target language system which is being simplified but that of the mother tongue,* i.e. that which is already known; and the simplification is towards some basic universal language-neutral natural semantax, which represents the starting point for second language acquisition.

Note

1   Just what is to be considered *simplicity* in the case of a grammar is a matter on which linguists are notoriously mealy-mouthed. One must, of course, distinguish the structural simplicity of a particular code from the simplicity in the description of grammars in general; in other words, it has nothing to do with the evaluation of grammars, or simplicity metrics. In spite of the unwillingness of linguists to commit themselves, there are fairly generally agreed structural features of a grammar which qualify it for being designated simple. The best available discussion of these is in Mühlhäusler (1974). Simplicity is, of course, an *overall* characteristic of a code. Thus, subsystems of a particular language may be simple by comparison with comparable subsystems in another language, but such simplicity may be counterbalanced by relative complexity elsewhere, e.g. in the lexical component.

Simplicity appears to be of two sorts: relative *poverty* (sometimes referred to by the 'process' terms *impoverishment* or *reduction*, Hymes 1971, Samarin 1971). By this is meant the absence of some feature found in other languages and not compensated for elsewhere in the system. The most obvious level of poverty is in the vocabulary, but another clear area is in the paucity of 'stylistic' paraphrases, i.e. alternative ways of saying the same thing, realized as relatively fixed word order, absence of passive construction, extraposition, clefting, etc. The overall effect of *poverty* is to reduce the range of possible messages transmittable by means of the code and the types of discourse which the code can serve: what Hymes (1971) calls *restriction*. *Simplicity* proper in a code is measured in terms of the degree of *regularity* in the grammar. This is seen most clearly in the morphological system, where the vocabulary of grammatical morphemes is small and the marking of concord and rection may be absent. The second simplicity feature is the more regular correspondence between content and expression. This can occur at the syntactic level where each semantic notion receives only one surface realization if any at all, and at the lexical level in a great increase of 'transparency' in lexical items and a preference for analytic rather than synthetic structures. The third simplicity feature is the relative absence of marked categories (cf. Hyltenstam

1978). This is especially clearly seen at the phonological level where the concept of markedness is more easily demonstrated.

In transformational terms many of these features show themselves as a greatly simplified transformational component in the grammar (Meisel 1977).

Bibliography

Bailey, C-J. and **R. W. Shuy** (eds.) (1973). *New Ways of Analysing Variation in English*. Washington: Georgetown University Press.

Bailey, N., C. Madden, and **S. Krashen** (1974). 'Is there a "natural sequence" in adult second language learning?' *Language Learning*, Vol. 24 No. 2, 235–243.

Bellugi, V. and **R. Brown** (eds.) (1968). *The Acquisition of Language*. Monograph of the Society for Research in Child Development, Vol. 29 No. 1.

Bickerton, D. (1975). *Dynamics of a Creole System*. Cambridge: Cambridge University Press.

Bickerton, D. (1977). 'Language Acquisition and Language Universals' in Valdman 1977b.

Boomer, D. S. and **J. M. Laver** (1968). 'Slips of the tongue'. *British Journal of Disorders of Communication*, Vol. 3 No. 1.

Brown, R. W. and **C. Frazer** (1964). 'The Acquisition of Syntax' in Bellugi and Brown 1968.

Brown, R. (1977). 'Talking to Children: Language Input and Output' in Snow and Ferguson 1977.

Burt, M. and **H. Dulay** (1974). 'A New Perspective on the Creative Construction Process in Child Second Language Acquisition'. *Working Papers in Bilingualism* 4, 71–98. Toronto: Ontario Institute for Studies in Education.

Carroll, J. B. (1955). *The Study of Language*. Cambridge: Harvard University Press.

Carroll, J. B. (1966). *Research in Foreign Language Teaching: The Last Five Years*. Report of the North East Conference on the Teaching of Foreign Languages 1966.

Cave, G. N. (1970). 'Some sociolinguistic factors in the production of standard language in Guyana'. *Language Learning*, Vol. 20 No. 2, 249–63.

Chomsky, N. (1966). *Research on Language Learning and Linguistics*. Report of the North East Conference 1966.

Clyne, M. (1968). 'Zum Pidgin-Deutsch der Gastarbeiter'. *Zeitschrift für Mundartforschung*, Vol. 35, 130–139.

Corder, S. P. (1973). *Introducing Applied Linguistics*. Harmondsworth: Penguin.

Corder, S. P. (1977a). 'The Language of Kehaar'. *RELC Journal*, Vol. 8, No. 1, 1–12.

Corder, S. P. and **E. Roulet** (eds.) (1977b). *Actes du Vème Colloque de Linguistique Appliqué de Neuchâtel*. Geneva; Droz et Université de Neuchâtel.

De Camp, D. (1971). 'Towards a Generative Analysis of a Post-Creole Speech Community' in Hymes 1971.

Dickerson, L. J. (1975). 'The learner's language as a system of variable rules'. *TESOL Quarterly*, Vol. 9 No. 4, 401–407.

Dulay, H. and **M. Burt** (1972). 'Goofing: an indication of children's second language learning strategies'. *Language Learning*, Vol. 22 No. 2, 235–51.

Dulay, H. and **M. Burt** (1973). 'Should we teach children syntax?' *Language Learning*, Vol. 23 No. 2, 245–258.

Dulay, H. and **M. Burt** (1974). 'Natural sequences in child second language acquisition'. *Language Learning*, Vol. 24 No. 1, 37–53.

Entwhistle, W. I. (1936). *The Spanish Language*. London: Faber and Faber.

Ervin-Tripp, S. (1974). 'Is second language learning like the first?' *TESOL Quarterly*, Vol. 8 No. 2, 111–129.

Ferguson, C. A. (1964). 'Baby Talk in Six Languages' in Gumperz and Hymes 1964.

Ferguson, C. A. (1966). *Research on Language Learning: Applied Linguistics*. Report of the North East Conference 1966.

Ferguson, C. A. (1971). 'Absence of the Copula and the Notion of Simplicity' in Hymes 1971.

Ferguson, C. A. and **D. Slobin** (eds.) (1973). *Studies of Child Language Development*. New York: Holt, Rinehart and Winston.

Ferguson, C. A. (1975). 'Towards a characterisation of English foreigner talk'. *Anthropological Linguistics*, 17, 1–14.

Ferguson, C. A. and **C. E. De Bose** (1977). 'Simplified Registers, Broken Language and Pidginization' in Valdman 1977b.

Fodor, J. A. and **J. J. Katz** (eds.) (1964). *The Structure of Language*. Englewood Cliffs, New Jersey: Prentice Hall.

Gaies, S. J. (1978). 'The Nature of Linguistic Input in Formal Second Language Learning'. *On TESOL 77*, 204–212. Washington: TESOL.

Gumperz, J. and **D. Hymes** (eds.) (1964). 'The ethnography of communication'. *American Anthropologist*, 66, 6, part 2. Washington: American Anthropological Association.

Hall, R. A. (1966). *Pidgin and Creole Language*. Ithaca: Cornell University Press.

Hatch, E. and **J. Wagner-Gough** (1976a). 'Explaining Sequence and Variation in Second Language Acquisition' in Brown, D. (ed.). *Papers in Second Language Acquisition. Language Learning* Special Issue No. 4.

Hatch, E., R. Shapiro, and **J. Gough** (1976b). 'Foreigner Talk Discourse'. Paper given at USC-UCLA Second Language Acquisition Forum 1976.

Hatch, E. (1978). 'Discourse Analysis and Second Language Acquisition' in Hatch, E. (ed.). *Second Language Acquisition.* Rowley: Newbury House.

Henzl, V. (1974). 'Linguistic register of foreign language instruction'. *Language Learning*, Vol. 23, No. 2, 207–22.

Henzl, V. (1975). 'Speech of Foreign Language Teachers: A Sociolinguistic Register Analysis'. Paper given at the fourth AILA Congress, Stuttgart 1975.

Hockett, C. F. (1948). 'A note on "structure"' in Joos, M. (ed.). *Readings in Linguistics.* University of Wisconsin Press.

Hyltenstam, K. (1977). 'Implicational patterns in interlanguage syntax variation'. *Language Learning*, Vol. 27 No. 2, 383–411.

Hyltenstam, K. (1978). 'A Framework for the Study of Interlanguage Continua'. *Working Papers No. 18.* Department of General Linguistics, University of Lund.

Hymes, D. (ed.) (1971). Introduction to Section III *Pidginization and Creolization of Languages.* Cambridge: Cambridge University Press, 63–90.

Jakobson, R. (1956). 'Two aspects of Language and Two Types of Aphasic Disturbance' in *Fundamentals in Language.* The Hague: Mouton.

Jakobson, R. (1968). *Child Language, Aphasia and Phonological Universals.* New York Humanities Press, 16–17.

James, C. (1971). 'Foreign Language Learning by Dialect Expansion'. Paper read to PAKS Symposium, Stuttgart 1971.

James, C. (1974). 'Linguistic measures for error gravity'. *AVLA Journal*, Vol. 12 No. 1, 3–9.

Katz, J. J. (1964). 'Semi-Sentences' in Fodor and Katz 1964.

Kay, P. and **G. Sankoff** (1972). 'A Language Universal Approach to Pidgins and Creoles'. *23rd Georgetown Roundtable on Language and Linguistics.* Georgetown University Press.

Kellerman, E. (1977). 'Towards the characterisation of the strategy of transfer in second language learning'. *Interlanguage Studies Bulletin,* Vol. 2 No. 1, 58–146.

Krashen, S. (1977). 'Some Issues Relating to the Monitor Model' in *On TESOL 1977.* Washington: TESOL.

Lado, R. (1961). *Linguistics Across Cultures.* Ann Arbor: University of Michigan Press.

Lambert, W. A. (1966). *Some Observations on First Language Acquisition and Second Language Learning.* (Mimeograph).

Larsen-Freeman, D. (1975). 'The acquisition of grammatical morphemes by adult second language students', *TESOL Quarterly,* Vol. 9 No. 4, 409–419.

Lenneberg, E. H. (ed.) (1966). *New Directions in the Study of Language.* Cambridge: M.I.T. Press.

Lenneberg, E. H. (1967). *The Biological Foundations of Language.* New York: Wiley.

Levenston, E. A. (1971). 'Overindulgence and Underrepresentation – Aspects of Mother Tongue Interference' in Nickel 1971.

Lyons, J. (1968). *Introduction to Theoretical Linguistics.* Cambridge: Cambridge University Press.

Lyons, J. (1972). 'Human Language' in Hinde, R. A. (ed.). *Non-Verbal Communication.* Cambridge: Cambridge University Press.

Lyons, J. (1973). 'Deixis as a Source of Reference'. *Work in Progress No. 6.* Department of Linguistics, University of Edinburgh.

McNeill, D. (1966). 'Developmental Psycholinguistics' in Smith and Miller 1966.

Mager, R. F. (1961). 'On the sequencing of instructional content'. *Psychological Reports 1961,* 405–12.

Meisel, J. (1977). 'Linguistic Simplification: A Study of Workers' Speech and Foreigner Talk' in Corder and Roulet 1977.

Miller, G. A. (1964). 'The psycholinguists'. *Encounter,* Vol. 23 No. 1, 29–37.

Miller, G. A. (1966). 'Language and Psychology' in Lenneberg 1966b.

Mühlhäusler, P. (1974). 'Pidginization and Simplification of Language'. *Pacific Linguistic Series:* B26. Australian National University.

Nemser, W. (1971). 'Approximative systems of foreign language learners'. *IRAL,* Vol. 9 No. 2, 115–123.

Newmark, L. (1966). 'How not to interfere with language learning'. *International Review of American Linguistics,* 40, 77–83.

Newport, E. L., H. Gleitman, and **L. R. Gleitman** (1977). 'Some Effects and Non-Effects of Maternal Speech Style' in Snow and Ferguson 1977.

Nickel, G. (ed.) (1971). *Contrastive Linguistics.* Cambridge: Cambridge University Press.

Nickel, G. (1973). 'Aspects of Error Analysis and Grading' in Svartvik 1973.

Palmer, H. E. (1917). *The Principles of Language Study*. Reprinted in *Language and Language Learning*. Oxford: Oxford University Press 1964.

Perkins, K. and **D. L. Freeman** (1975). 'The effect of formal language instruction on the order of morpheme acquisition'. *Language Learning*, Vol. 25, No. 2, 237–243.

Reibel, D. A. (1969). 'What to do with Recalcitrant Relatives'. Paper given at the Linguistic Association of Great Britain meeting April 1969.

Richards, J. C. (1971). 'Error analysis and second language strategies'. *Language Science*, Vol. 17, 12–22.

Richards, J. C. (1974). 'Simplification: a Strategy in Adult Acquisition of a Foreign Language'. Paper given at the Second Conference on the Standardization of Languages, Manila 1974.

Samarin, W. J. (1971). 'Salient and Substantive Pidgins' in Hymes 1971.

Saporta, S. (1966). 'Applied Linguistics and Generative Grammar' in Valdman 1966.

Schatz, M. and **R. Gelman** (1977). 'Beyond Syntax: The Influence of Conversational Constraints on Speech Modification' in Snow and Ferguson 1977.

Schumann, J. H. (1975). 'Implication of Pidginization and Creolization for the Study of Adult Second Language Acquisition' in Schumann and Stenson 1975.

Schumann, J. H. and **N. Stenson** (eds.) (1975). *New Frontiers in Second Language Learning*. Rowley: Newbury House.

Selinker, L. (1969). 'Language transfer'. *General Linguistics*, Vol. 9 No. 2, 67–92.

Selinker, L. (1972). 'Interlanguage'. *IRAL*, Vol. 10 No. 3, 219–31.

Slobin, D. (1973). 'Cognitive Prerequisites for the Acquisition of Grammar' in Ferguson and Slobin 1973.

Smith, F. and **G. A. Miller** (eds.) (1966). *The Genesis of Language*. Cambridge: M.I.T. Press.

Snow, C. E. and **C. A. Ferguson** (1977). *Talking to Children: Language Input and Acquisition*. Cambridge: Cambridge University Press.

Spolsky, B. (1966). 'A psycholinguistic critique of programmed foreign language instruction'. *IRAL*, Vol. 4 No. 2, 119–29.

Svartvik, J. (ed.) (1973). *Errata: Papers in Error Analysis*. Lund: Gleerup.

Tarone, E., A. D. Cohen, and **G. Dumas** (1976). 'A closer look at some interlanguage terminology: a framework for communication strategies'. *Working Papers in Bilingualism* 9, 76–91. Toronto: Ontario Institute for Studies in Education.

Taylor, B. (1975). 'The use of overgeneralisation and transfer learning strategies by elementary and intermediate students in ESL'. *Language Learning*, Vol. 25 No. 1, 73–107.

Thorne, J. B. (1965). 'Stylistics and generative grammars'. *Journal of Linguistics*, Vol. 1 No. 1, 49–59.

Traugott, E. (1973). 'Some Thoughts on Natural Syntactic Processes' in Bailey and Shuy 1973.

Traugott, E. (1977). 'Natural Semantax: Its Role in the Study of Second Language Acquisition' in Corder and Roulet 1977.

Tsuzaki, S. M. (1971). 'Coexistent Systems in Language Variation' in Hymes 1971.

Valdman, A. (ed.) (1966). *Trends in Modern Language Teaching.* New York: McGraw-Hill.

Valdman, A. (1977a). 'Elaboration in Creole French Dialects' in Valdman 1977b.

Valdman, A. (1977b). *Pidgin and Creole Linguistics.* Bloomington: Indiana University Press.

Valdman, A. (1978). 'On the relevance of the pidginization-creolization model for second language learning'. *Studies in Second Language Acquisition*, Vol. 1 No. 2, 55–77.

Varadi, T. (1973). 'Strategies of Target Language Communications: Message Adjustment'. Paper given at the sixth Conference of Rumania-English Project, Timisoara 1973.

Whinnom, K. (1971). 'Linguistic Hybridization' in Hymes 1971.

Widdowson, H. G. (1977). 'The significance of simplification'. *Studies in Second Language Acquisition*, Vol. 1 No. 1, 11–21.

Widdowson, H. G. (1978). *Teaching Language as Communication.* Oxford: Oxford University Press.